How to Drive
LIKE A **CHRISTIAN**

A Lighthearted Guide to Success on
the Highway and on the Road of Life

T E R R I   C O X

ISBN: 978-1-4834-9484-5 (sc)
ISBN: 978-1-4834-9483-8 (e)

Library of Congress Control Number: 2018914533

Lulu Publishing Services rev. date: 01/03/2019

Dedicated to my husband, Chip, who is my
favorite companion on the road of life.

CONTENTS

Chapter 1   Losing Your Religion 1
Chapter 2   Welcome to the Road.. 5
Chapter 3   Avoiding Distractions 9
Chapter 4   Pet Peeves 13
Chapter 5   Fellow Travelers 17
Chapter 6   Bumper Stickers.. 21
Chapter 7   Stuck in Traffic 24
Chapter 8   Curves Ahead 27
Chapter 9   Intersections—Part I.. 30
Chapter 10   Intersections—Stop and Go.. 34
Chapter 11   Sightseeing.. 38
Chapter 12   Struggling Up the Hill.. 41
Chapter 13   Maintenance.. 46
Chapter 14   Parking Lots 50
Chapter 15   Fender Benders 55
Chapter 16   Speed Limits... 59
Chapter 17   Directions... 63
Chapter 18   Stormy Weather 67
Chapter 19   Arriving Safely at Home 71

Scripture References.. 75
About the Author.. 83

CHAPTER 1

Losing Your Religion

Doris had just finished Bible study and was walking out to the parking lot. Brother Bob, the study leader (and a pillar of the church) was getting into his car. "Oh, I just remembered, Brother Bob," Doris called out. "Ted dropped me off tonight so he could use the car to pick up the kids at play practice. Do you mind giving me a ride home?"

"Of course not," he answered. "We can continue our discussion on James, chapter 3."

As they pulled out of the parking lot, Bob said, "This is great. We have time for a few more minutes of exhortation."

"I really appreciated your point during Bible study," said Doris, "that the tongue is such a small part of the body, but it can do such great damage."

"Yes, and those of us who are willing to call ourselves Christians are under constant scrutiny by the unsaved," said Brother Bob. "It takes great restraint and constant diligence to keep our speech pure. As James put it 'No one can tame the tongue, it is a restless evil and full of deadly'... What in the Sam Hill, you crazy imbecile!"

"Excuse me?" yelled Doris as Brother Bob slammed on the brakes.

"That crazy moron!" He yelped. "Right there in the white SUV! Didn't you see him cut me off! The nerve of that insane Tasmanian devil! Who does he think he is anyway! He probably learned to drive in a demolition derby..."

"Bob! Bob! Settle down," Doris soothed. "We're okay! I believe that was a four-way stop back there. The SUV had the right-of-way."

"Well, that may be so, but those big gas-guzzlers always try to hog the road." Bob's decibel level was returning to normal.

"My, my. You just gave a marvelous example of the scripture we were discussing," Doris said with a slight chuckle.

"What do you mean?" Bob replied defensively.

"Taming the tongue? I believe you were about to complete the quote 'The tongue is a restless evil and full of deadly... poison.'"

"Oh, that!" Bob laughed. "I'm sure brother James never had to drive in traffic with all of these untrained hooligans. He was writing a letter to the early church. They never had to contend with SUV's and teenage drivers and women who..."

"Women who what?" Doris asked with eyebrows raised.

"Oh you know. Never mind," Bob replied hesitantly. "Ah, here we are," he lilted while pulling into Doris's driveway. "I'll see you next week at Bible study. We'll be continuing in James 3, where it says, 'the wisdom from above is first pure, then peaceable, gentle, and so on.'"

Doris got out of the car and just stood in the driveway with her mouth hanging open, waving speechlessly.

*****

It has always fascinated me how emotions are intensified when you get into the driver's seat of a car. All of the things your mother taught you growing up, all of the tenets of the Bible, all of the objectives for positive thinking come to a head when putting the car into drive. While standing in the parking lot with your car keys in hand, all is joviality and camaraderie, but as soon as the key turns in the ignition, it is "Every man (or woman) for himself!"

Take the case of Brother Bob, for example. If Brother Bob and I had been walking from the Bible classroom and encountered SUV Man at the juncture of the education wing and the choir suite, Bob would have smiled warmly and waved SUV Man by with a cheery blessing. But put the same two individuals in vehicles on the open road, and it becomes a case of Jekyll and Hyde! Bob is no longer sweetness and light. He no longer has the best interest of his neighbor at heart. Brotherly love is tossed out the window, and the road becomes a battleground for dominance of the asphalt.

So what causes the mystical transformation that takes place while climbing behind the wheel? Why do we view our fellow man in such a different light through the windshield of a car?

Perhaps it is the fact that the roadway is a common ground for all people--people who are much like you and people who are, in every possible way, different from you. They are all there and are in a very big hurry to get somewhere, just like you. Or maybe they are not in enough of a hurry to please you.

The other problem with relating to other drivers is just that—you can't relate to them. For example, if you would like to say, "Excuse me, Lady In The Blue Pick-up Truck, but would you please wait until I pass by before pulling out into the road," it just isn't possible. She can't hear you. And even if she could, she doesn't know you. She doesn't know that you are heading to an important dentist appointment. She has her own priorities. She has waited what she deemed to be an inordinately long time to enter the roadway. She saw this as her big chance to enter the fray and made her way to pick up her children from daycare, and she was late.

You see how difficult relating to other drivers can be?

That is assuming that you are concerned about the other drivers on the road. Maybe you are not concerned about them at all. Maybe you see them as an annoying hindrance to the progress towards your destination. Herein lies the challenge. How do you drive like a Christian? As Brother Bob stated, Jesus and the apostles did not have to contend with rush-hour traffic on the interstate. So how can my Christian faith apply to this modern situation?

In I Corinthians 10:13, the Apostle Paul says, "No temptation has overtaken you but such as is common to man: and God is faithful, who will not allow you to be tempted beyond what you are able, but with the temptation will provide the way of escape also, that you may be able to endure it.(The New International Version)." This reminds us that Christ has provided us with whatever we need to be victorious and resist evil, even when driving amongst the unwashed masses. There is no temptation that people have not had to cope with in the past. The setting may be a little different, but the temptation to sin is the same. God is not limited by time or technology. His truths apply to all challenges—past, present, and future.

So do not despair! God has equipped you to handle the frustrations of the roadway and arrive victoriously at your appointed destination. Not only that, He may surprise you with what you can learn while on the way. As we often have been told, a journey from point A to point B is often a metaphor for our pathway through life. You start out. You encounter irritating distractions, fellow travelers, and curves in the road. There are choices to be made at each intersection. And, hopefully, you will arrive safe at home. Each of these experiences can be a lesson in life and love. So let's explore some of these and find out how driving like a Christian can make a difference.

CHAPTER 2

Welcome to the Road

When your fifteen-year-old son receives his learner's permit, your stress level reaches a new high.

"This is great! Now I can hang out with my friends whenever I want. I don't have to listen to that lame stuff you always play on the radio, 'cause everyone knows that the driver controls the radio. Exactly how fast will a mini-van go, anyway? You'll have to tell me when to turn 'cause I've never really noticed how we get anywhere we're going..."

"Whoa! Slow down, tiger," I caution. "We haven't even left the DMV parking lot yet! There are a lot of things we have to go over first. Now get out of the driver's seat and let me drive home. We'll start you out in the church parking lot when no one else is around."

"Oh, Mom! You really know how to take all the fun out of a perfectly awesome situation," he moans.

To a new teenaged driver, the space inside an automobile seems to be a brave new world. He anticipates freedom beyond his imagination. He is about to enter into a world where he is in control of where he goes, how he gets there, when he arrives, and who he takes with him. There is nothing worse than having Mom and Dad waiting in the parking lot, anxious to get back home after a school basketball game. You want to hang out by the door pretending to be talking to another guy, when you are really waiting to accidentally bump into that girl who noticed you in the gym. Mom and Dad are blowing the horn and motioning you over and you're trying to make an impression. Now with your driver's license in sight, you will be free to "chill" and "hang out" as much as you want!

But back to reality. It's time for that first practice session in the church parking lot. You get in the driver's seat and put on your seatbelt. That should please Mom. You turn on the ignition. Check your mirrors. Look around you for other cars. Now you are ready. You turn on the radio and begin to scroll through stations, looking for the perfect jam for your ride.

"What are you doing?" I ask.

"Just picking out some good music for a change," he replies.

"Hold on there, buster. You won't be doing that for quite a while," I say.

"What do you mean?" he cries in disbelief. He has waited a lifetime to do this.

"It will be too much of a distraction," I reply with a no-nonsense tone.

"Are you kidding? I listen to this all the time. I eat, drink, and breathe music. It won't possibly be a distraction!" he says, pleading his case.

"Son, driving is a new experience for you. It is going to take every ounce of concentration you have and then some. Not only will the music distract you, but what if you decide you want to change the station while driving? If you take your eyes off that road for even a second, it could mean your life or death and even the life of others on the road," I remind him.

"I guess I didn't think about that. I don't really think so, but ..."

"Just take my word for it, Son. Driving is not just a walk in the park. It is a very big responsibility and can be very dangerous if not taken seriously," I say. "And that goes for eating while driving, goofing off with your friends, waving at someone out the window, reaching down for something in the floorboard, any number of things. I can't count all of the times I have heard someone say they took their eyes off the road for just a second and ended up in a serious accident."

"Yeah, okay. I get it. So what do I do first?" he asks, ready to get on with the lesson.

"Check all around, put the gear in drive, and ease down on the gas pedal," I say helpfully.

"Okay, here goes… Wait, I didn't mean to do that… what happened?"

"It's okay. You didn't hit anything," I say.

"What did I do?"

"Well, first of all, you hit the gas pedal with a little too much force," I reply.

"And what else?"

"You were in reverse."

*****

Do you remember what it was like when you first gave your heart to Christ? You were so excited about your faith. You wanted to rush into the world and share the good news of what Christ had done for you. Or maybe you grew up in the church and felt as if you always knew Him. Then one day you realized that it was time to make a commitment and tell the world that you wanted to follow Him. It's like the new teen driver. He is ready to go racing out of the DMV parking lot and tear down the road with the music blasting…except for one thing. He's not quite sure where the "drive" gear is. He doesn't know the rules of the road or even where he is going.

A new Christian needs the help of other more experienced brothers and sisters in Christ to show the way. He needs to put the key in the ignition—connect with God, the power source. He must start out slowly with a guide who will never steer him wrong—The Holy Spirit—and stay in constant prayer. He must apply the lessons learned in the driving manual—God's Word. Then with daily experience, he will learn to drive through life, one trip at a time.

Now I realize that you may not be new to driving. You could be a novice, but perhaps you have been driving since rumble seats were in fashion. Either way, think of today as the first day of the rest of your driving career. You are all shiny and new!

Seriously, if you have found that driving brings out the anger in you, take this opportunity to turn this over to God. Just as when you first made your commitment to Christ, you can admit your sin and ask for God's forgiveness. Is this language too strong for you? Am I overemphasizing the situation? Why, everyone gets angry when driving!

Yes, driving brings out strong emotions, and you must stay sharp and focused when on the road. But you cannot use that as an excuse to lose control. Driving can reveal something inside that is not entirely surrendered to God's control. Just as the new driver taking instruction from a loving parent, you can learn to drive in a new way by allowing the Father to guide you. Surrender your emotions to Him.

First of all, focus on what is important. Let God guide you on your drive. Look at the drive ahead as an opportunity to trust God and be open to what He has in store for you. Expect the unexpected and see it as a way for God to open you to something new. The irritations that irked you before may become a chance for God to use you.

Remember *Where's Waldo?* How you scanned the pages looking intently for that little guy in the striped shirt? On your next drive, look for God in the same way. You will find Him in the most unlikely places. Just as it says in Deuteronomy 4:29 "But if from there you seek the Lord your God, you will find Him if you seek him with all your heart and with all your soul."

CHAPTER 3

Avoiding Distractions

Im drvng 2 grocre str. Anythg u want?
  Out of mlk
  Ok. Whats 4 supr?
  U tell me
  ?
  Oops
  Lol. Ran off rd. 2 bz textng
  Ok?
  Ys. Oops
  ?

Blu lites.

"Good evening, officer."

*****

There are many things that can distract you when driving. Sometimes it amazes me to see what people do in their cars. Once I was waiting at a red light, and another car slammed into the rear of my car. I jerked forward and was pretty shaken up. I was waiting for the other driver to come and check on me, but she didn't even get out of her car. I got myself together, climbed out of the driver's seat and walked back to her. She had backed up and was sitting there as if nothing had happened. I went up to the window.

"Ma'am, are you okay?" I asked.

"Oh yes," she said.

"What happened?" I asked, my voice rising.

"Oh, that! Me and my kids were all eating ice cream cones. I just wasn't paying attention," she giggled.

"Don't you think we should look at the damage or call the police?" I asked.

"Oh, no. I'm sure everything's okay," she answered while leaning over the back of the seat. "Henry, you sit down and behave!"

I looked at my bumper and decided she was probably right, but asked for her insurance information anyway. At that point, it was not so much the damage to the car, but the fact that she had no regard for my feelings or my health, that mattered.

Ice cream, misbehaving children, eating, drinking, radios, text-messaging, applying make-up, the sports page—the list goes on. That's not to mention the distractions taking place outside the car. Road work, weather, crazy drivers, kids on bicycles, rush-hour traffic—it never ends. How can a person concentrate on safe driving with so many things going on at once? One must remember the great responsibility we take into our hands each time we activate the speeding missile that is an automobile. We must think of each life we will encounter along the way as well as our own lives.

You can eat ice cream any time. You know, you probably don't need it anyway.

You can pull over to discipline the children. Haven't you ever heard a parent say, "If you don't stop that, I'm going to pull this car over!" You may be a little late for an appointment, but it's very effective.

We all managed to struggle through and communicate just fine before there were cell phones. You can put off that call until later.

Just consider the possible consequences.

And as far as the outside distractions, why not put all of that great video game skill to good use. You can get to your goal by concentrating on the road instead of the distractions around you. And you will get lots of points for getting there safely.

I'll never forget the first time I took my son to the pediatrician. I was ready to answer all of his questions about my son's health and safety. I was very surprised when his first question to me was "Are you wearing *your* seatbelt every time you drive?"

I answered affirmatively, but asked why he wanted to know.

"This little boy needs his mother," he replied. "Remember that every time you get behind the wheel. It's not just about you anymore."

That's the point. It's not just about you when you are driving. It's about everyone along the way. You can change the lives of those around you by concentrating completely on the responsibility of controlling your vehicle. The same applies if you give in to distractions. One little slip, and a catastrophe could happen. I actually had to give up praying while driving. I would get too involved and forget where I was going!

***

In our spiritual walk, there can be two kinds of distractions. There can actually be a useful kind. We may be travelling full-speed in the wrong direction. God does not always lead us along the path we expect. Life is not always a journey along a well-paved road. It is more like a "spaghetti junction" of intersecting roads with lots of merging and yielding. If we become focused on the wrong thing, a distraction may be necessary in order to help us to look in a new direction. As it says in Isaiah 55:8, "'For my thoughts are not your thoughts, neither are your ways my ways,' declares the Lord."

Next time you're in a rut, so to speak, be on the lookout for a distraction. It may be just what you need to get your spirit out of first gear and onto a road leading just where God means for you to go.

And then there are the detrimental sorts of distractions. As we speed along our way through life, it is easy to be distracted by many things. The Bible has quite a few things to say on this subject.

In Hebrews Chapter 12, the author compares our Christian journey to a race, or a drive in the car, as it were.

"Therefore, since we are surrounded by such a great cloud of witnesses, let us throw off everything that hinders and the sin that so easily entangles. And let us run with perseverance the race marked out for us, fixing our eyes on Jesus, the pioneer and perfecter of faith. For the joy set before him he endured the cross, scorning its shame, and sat down at the right hand of the throne of God. Consider him who endured such opposition from sinners, so that you will not grow weary and lose heart." Hebrews 12:1-3

We should lay aside the distractions in life that keep us from achieving all that God wants us to accomplish. He aptly mentions that sin easily entangles us, as do the irritating actions of other drivers on the highway. We get caught up in the frustration so easily. It happens in our homes, schools, sports complexes, workplaces, and even in our churches. We allow fruitless anger to sway us from our goal.

And, just for the record, what is that goal? There are so many things to which we should aspire. Well, Jesus summed it up easily when the Pharisees asked him which of the hundreds of godly rules was most important. "Love the Lord, your God, with all your heart and soul and mind, and love your neighbor as yourself." (Matthew. 22:37-39) Focus fully on that goal, and the distractions will sort themselves out!

CHAPTER FOUR

Pet Peeves

Everyone has pet peeves when it comes to driving. Yeah, you just thought of yours. Here's one of mine.

You're cruising down the two-lane highway at a healthy pace, passing side roads every now and then. Up ahead you see a car pull up to a stop sign.

"No. I don't believe it. You're not going to pull out in front of me, are you? Surely, you're not pulling...you're pulling out! Yep, I knew it. Not only are you pulling out in front of me, but you're going twenty-five miles an hour. That's okay. I didn't have anywhere to go anyway. What are you do-ing? How can your car possibly go that slowly? We're not in a parade, you know. Maybe I can pass. What am I thinking? There's not one stretch of road for the next twenty miles with a place to pass. I'll just ride his bumper and lay on the horn. Maybe that will speed him up. Okay, I knew it. He pulled out in front of me, drove for a quarter mile, and now he's turning off. Well, at least he'll be out of the way."

"Hey, I know who that is. It's Harvey. Yeah, and Harvey's wife. What is she, about nine months pregnant? I remember when I was that pregnant. I would fuss at my husband whenever he went over a bump or turned a curve. I guess that's why Harvey's driving like that. Now they're turning into the convenience store. She probably has a craving for chocolate milk and circus peanuts. Guess I'll have to cut him some slack."

***

That's the thing. When you're driving and someone else gets on your last nerve, it's never simple. There are a million and one reasons why someone is driving erratically. But you can bet your boots that they are not motivated by a desire to drive you insane. They have their own reasons and motivations for what they are doing, and it has very little or nothing to do with you. So don't take it so personally. Remember, we all act as if the world revolves around us. You do, and so does the other guy. Have patience, most traffic irritations are temporary.

Here's another one. Why does everyone slow down to look when there is an accident? Around here, we call them "Looky Lous". You know—rubberneckers. The traffic has already slowed down! Now you are making it even worse! Admit it. You want to see some wreckage—human or mechanical. We humans like to see other people's wreckage. Wrecked relationships, dysfunctional families, people with higher credit card bills than ours. It makes us feel better about our own frailties. And it applies to driving as well. "Look at how that fellow pulled out in front of me! I'd never do that!" Of course not.

Be honest. You have wrecked at some point--on the road or in your life. Why not give the other guy a break. Focus on your own driving, and maybe you'll avoid the swerve up ahead.

And what about those old fogies who insist on riding in the passing lane on the interstate—going 40 miles per hour? What are they thinking? Why get in that lane in the first place? It's just as dangerous to go too slowly in the passing lane as it is to drive too fast-- probably more so. Especially since that pushes my road rage buttons!

Maybe it's not really an old lady at all. Maybe it's an angel in disguise, keeping you from going too fast. Maybe if you hadn't had to slow down, you would have gotten into an accident up ahead. I've heard stories. You know—one Wednesday night no one makes it to choir practice on time at the church because there is an accident and the road is closed. Right at time for choir practice, ka-boom! The old boiler in the church explodes. Everyone is saved! And just a few minutes ago they were all complaining about the traffic.

Then there are the times when you are waiting in the left-turning lane behind another driver. You know that when the light turns green that there won't be much time to make your move. Depending on the timing of the intersection there will be three or four drivers, at the most, who will make it. So, now it's time, the light is about to change, and... it's green. Okay, man-- go, go, go! Like, right now! What are you waiting for? We're about to miss our window. What the heck are you doing up there? Oh, man, he's on his cell phone! I'll honk the horn. Good, he's moving! Aaaand, it's red. Dang it!

Naw, I don't think that one was an angel. Boy, that really ticks me off! I can feel my blood boiling. I need to take a deep breath. I'm going to find it really hard to get that "Kum Bah Yah" feeling this time, no matter how hard I'm trying to have a Christian attitude. No, I don't feel like loving my neighbor just now.

*****

How can a Christian maintain his religion with all these people getting on your last nerve? First of all, you have to admit to yourself that most of the pet peeve situations are not a matter of life and death. They are annoying and irritating, but in the long run, they usually only cause minor delays. As crazy as it sounds, you can easily take a moment to pray for those around you: the guy who pulls out in front of you, the one who is talking on the cell phone, the granny in the fast lane--whoever. You can re-channel all the energy you would have put into cursing your fellow motorist and use that to let God's power flow--into you and into those around you. Does that sound too simple? Most of God's truths are simple. We are the ones who make things complicated.

In his letter to the Ephesians, the apostle Paul encourages Christ's followers to "walk in a manner worthy of the calling with which you have been called, with humility and gentleness, with patience, showing forbearance to one another in love." (Ephesians. 4:1, 2) Just substitute 'drive' for 'walk'. Drive in a manner that would please the Lord, and be ready to forgive the other guys. That's forbearance—putting up with someone in love. Goodness knows, none of us is perfect when it comes to driving. Forgive one another, just as you would want the other driver to forgive you.

I know. Forgiving is hard. It's hard even when it's someone you know and love. Even when it's someone you know loves you. So how can you "love" some goofball on the road that you don't even know? Here's how— remember that love is not just a feeling. It's a choice you make. You choose to love-- to forgive the goofball behavior--not because you feel like it, but because God has commanded it. It's good for you and for those around you.

It's also often the case that the thing that enervates us most is something we do ourselves. Jesus said in Matthew 7, "And why do you look at the speck that is in your brother's eye, but do not notice the log that is in your own eye? Or how can you say to your brother, 'Let me take the speck out of your eye.' And behold, the log is in your own eye? You hypocrite, first take the log out of your own eye, and then you will see clearly to take the speck out of your brother's eye."

Here's an example.

Oh. Here we are at the stop sign. Man, there's a lot of traffic on the road today. Maybe I can pull out after this pickup goes by. Here we go— no, wait. I didn't see that Euro behind them. Maybe now—nope, here comes another train of cars from the other direction. I'll just have to pull out and punch the gas. Now!

Whoops. That guy behind me is so close. It'll take a few seconds to get up to speed. Okay, I'm almost there. He's crowding my tail. Dummy! Oh, there's my turn. I'd better signal. What's he blinking his headlights for? I had to pull out then, or I would never get a chance. I'll never understand why people ride my bumper. That's another pet peeve of mine.

CHAPTER 5

Fellow Travelers

You know, driving wouldn't be so bad were it not for all of the other people on the road. And I don't understand it either. I mean, most rules of driving are just common sense and good manners. Don't we all have a mom and dad who taught us these things? By the way everyone else drives, you would think they were all raised by a pack of wild hyenas with no regard for anyone else. That is, everyone except me. That's why I tried to teach my children the truth when they began driving.

"Expect everyone else on the road to be insane," I told them. "Don't trust anyone else. No one is really concentrating on their driving. They are all thinking about what they just did, or why they are late, or they are texting or talking on their cell phones, or yelling at the opposing political

17

party on the radio, or jamming to some excellent hip hop, or screaming at their kids in the back seat."

With that said, let's take a look at just who is sharing the road with us.

Teenage drivers—You can easily spot them. They are either riding the edge of the asphalt on the right shoulder, or veering towards the center line. They can't understand which lane to drive in and will change lanes without notice. They may have an adult in the passenger seat with a horrified expression.

The "highly seasoned" driver—This person has had a license since, well, before there were licenses! They have managed to retain their driving license due to the mail-in renewals. They clearly cannot see, hear, or maintain steady pressure on the gas pedal.

The mom-in-a-van—This vehicle has lots of bumper stickers: An old peeling sticker which once said "Baby on Board," "I visited Disney World," "My child is an honor roll student at City Elementary School," lots of soccer balls with names in them, and so on. This driver is frantically multi-tasking. She has just dropped off child #1 at practice and is passing out fruit snacks to child # 2 and the neighbor child she is picking up for another van-mom. She is talking to a friend on the phone and digging through book bags for homework assignments. Unlikely as it may sound, these moms do an amazingly good job of focusing. They are usually some of the best drivers on the road.

Cell phone addicts—When the light turns green, this person isn't going. They are driving consistently 40 mph on the interstate and swerving into your lane in oncoming traffic. When awakened by your blaring horn, they smile and wave with the non-cell-phone-holding hand.

The boomers-- Their music is so loud that it rattles the Coke cans inside your car. It makes your heart stop and your head ache. Do they think that everyone else likes their music? I would play my Broadway show tunes loud enough to bug them, but I can't afford the stereo equipment. Where did they get the money for all that stuff anyway? They're only 18 years old and work at the supermarket!

Tractors, cement trucks, 18-wheelers and other vehicle much larger than you-- Isn't there another route they could be taking?

And finally:

Other skilled law-abiding drivers just like you-- We drive only five miles over the speed limit (or ten on the highway.) We make eye contact at intersections and occasionally let people into traffic. We always look before we turn right on red and almost come to a full stop at a stop sign. Are any of you out there?

So, what should we think about those we meet on the road? The road is the great equalizer. There is every manner of person out there in some vehicle, going to their various destinations. They are men, women, and children. They are of every age and race. They hold to every religion or no religion. They are Christian or not. They are healthy or sick. Tired or energized. They may be singing. They may be cursing. They are all travelling at a high rate of speed in large, heavy machines that have the potential to do great damage and don't even consider that. And most are on automatic pilot, in their own little car-universes--not really paying much attention to their driving.

***

Jesus shared the road with all kinds of people, too. In fact, He was known for rubbing elbows with people that were not the elite. He sought out the sick, the despised, and the misunderstood. He didn't just ride along with the nice crowd, although He had a fine group of men (and women) who He travelled with daily.

As is the case with inexperienced drivers, He was not dismayed when encountering someone who didn't understand God's rules of the road. Once while travelling in Samaria, he encountered a woman drawing water at the town well. Normally, Jews would not have anything to do with Samaritans. But Jesus was not put off by someone unfamiliar with His message. The Samaritan woman said to him, "You are a Jew and I am a Samaritan woman. How can you ask me for a drink?" Jesus answered her, "If you knew the gift of God and who it is that asks you for a drink, you would have asked him and he would have given you living water." "Sir," the woman said, "you have nothing to draw with and the well is deep. Where can you get this living water? Are you greater than our father Jacob, who gave us the well and drank from it himself, as did also his sons and his livestock?" Jesus answered, "Everyone who drinks this water will be thirsty again, but whoever drinks the water I give them will never thirst. Indeed, the water I give them will become in them a spring of water welling up to eternal life." (John chapter 4)

Like the elder driver, He gave hope to those who had been seeking truth for many years like Simeon and Anna, the prophetess who saw God's promise come true at the temple when Jesus was a baby. Jesus's friend Martha could been seen as the multi-tasking mom, and like those on the cell phone, He had a clear message for the self-absorbed Pharisees. He was also known to stop in the middle of traffic and look in an unusual direction to find someone in need. (Remember Zaccheus?) He rode on a donkey instead of a steed, and he made some noise from time to time that disturbed the status quo. And though He was known to go seeking the lost, He cherished the faithful who truly followed Him with a pure heart.

And this is what Jesus encountered on the road. He saw all manner of people in every circumstance. Some adored Him, some reviled Him. Some hungered for His message or His touch. Some were puzzled by Him or amazed by Him. Some quickly recognized Him as God's Messiah, while others loudly denied His deity. No matter what was going on along the road or their reaction to Him, His reaction was the same. He saw past their circumstances and looked directly at their need. He ignored the outward distractions and spoke words to their hearts.

When you are dismayed by the masses of inattentive drivers, just remember, we're all on the road together, trying to get to our destinations. God may just put that person in your path today who needs an understanding smile from you, and he may be putting someone in your path who can help you.

So, as you encounter your fellow travelers along the road, consider the example of Christ. "Let all bitterness and wrath and anger and clamor and slander be put away from you, along with all malice. And be kind to one another, tenderhearted, forgiving each other, just as God in Christ also has forgiven you." (Ephesians. 4:31-32)

Honk if you love Jesus!

 If you don't like my driving, keep it to yourself.

CHAPTER 6

Bumper Stickers

When I was growing up, my dad never let us put a bumper sticker on our car. He was a newspaper man, so I think that he wanted to be seen as neutral on most topics. Plus my mom thought that bumper stickers were tacky. I've heard that attorneys ask potential jurors what bumper stickers are on their cars during voir dire. They can tell you a lot about what is important to a person.

If you are travelling behind a vehicle with multiple bumper stickers, it's fun to see if they develop a theme. The muddy 4-wheel drive truck might have an NRA sticker, various styles of deer heads, "Don't Tread on Me", and a sticker touting the second amendment. Another common grouping would be a soccer ball with the name Whitney on it, stick figures representing five family members and a dog, "My Kid is an Honor Student at CES", and "I'd Rather be at Disney World."

Other bumpers display slogans of favorite sports teams, various social issues, or support for political candidates on all levels. There are loads of these on each side of the fence, each as enthusiastic as the other, proving that we do, indeed, live in a diverse nation.

You rarely see bumper stickers with MENSA on them or "My Kid Graduated with a C Average." Neither do you see, "I may not be attractive, but I have strong character traits." Some ideas are better revealed on a more personal level—not on a bumper.

So why do people put stickers on their bumpers? As decoration? Are they merely proud of their accomplishments? Are they seeking to gain support of their causes? Do you expect the drivers around you to read your messages and to be affected by them? Are they looking for like-minded drivers who might want to pull over and share a conversation about social equality or "How 'Bout Them Dogs?"

As a Christian, I believe that you should put some thought into your bumper sticker profile. We know that whatever we do may be observed by other drivers as an example of how Christ would behave. Though He didn't drive a car, Jesus was out on the road, travelling among the people on a regular basis. He was constantly judged by those around Him. Though He didn't have a bumper promoting saintly slogans, His words were carefully scrutinized and shared one-to-one by the crowds. Often His words and actions were misconstrued or misunderstood. They were taken out of context and still are today.

I have joked many times with my Christian friends about hesitating to put a Christian-related sticker on my car. Even the most saintly driver might cut someone off or execute some driving maneuver that wouldn't be seen as Christ-like. Then the other drivers see your "Follow me to Fellowship Church" bumper sticker and shake their heads. "Bunch of hypocrites!" they might mumble. Whatever is stuck to our bumpers, Christians know that we are flawed and likely to make a mess of things, just as the next guy. The big difference is that we are forgiven, and by God's grace, we can overcome our failures.

***

That's the interesting thing about slogans—pithy statements that might fit on a bumper. The statements are hanging out there in space without a context. They might easily be misunderstood. Another person reading or hearing the phrase is open to interpret what they read however they wish. Important statements are much better understood when shared in person in a conversation with real people who are known to each other.

Jesus knew that people often take a simple statement of truth and try to twist it into something else. Though Jesus did address the masses, many of His most heart-changing words occurred one-on-one with people who were hungry to hear the truth. When the crowds began to twist His words, He made sure that they understood His motives.

In Luke 5, we read the account of a paralyzed man. The man's friends had let him down through the ceiling of the house in order to reach Jesus.

"When Jesus saw their faith, he said, "Friend, your sins are forgiven."

"The Pharisees and the teachers of the law began thinking to themselves, "Who is this fellow who speaks blasphemy? Who can forgive sins but God alone?"

Jesus knew what they were thinking and asked, "Why are you thinking these things in your hearts? Which is easier: to say, 'Your sins are forgiven,' or to say, 'Get up and walk'? But I want you to know that the Son of Man has authority on earth to forgive sins." So he said to the paralyzed man, "I tell you, get up, take your mat and go home." Immediately he stood up in front of them, took what he had been lying on and went home praising God. Everyone was amazed and gave praise to God. They were filled with awe and said, "We have seen remarkable things today." (Luke. 5:20-26)

Maybe bumper stickers are an interesting way to start a conversation, but rather than being a "bumper sticker Christian," get out of your comfort zone and share Christ's good words in meaningful conversation with others. Ask God to open the door to opportunities for interaction with the people in your world. One-to-one is the best way to share those ideas that really mean something to you.

CHAPTER 7

Stuck in Traffic

I have never envied my neighbors who have that long drive into the city every morning, commuting to a higher paying job than mine. Yes, the pay might be worth it to some, but I just can't stand being stuck in bumper to bumper traffic for hours. Of course, the commuters know the drill and what to expect. They know the exact mile marker and dot on the clock where the slowdowns will occur. They know how to get someone to let them into the proper lane at the proper time. It's predictable, if nothing else.

Some people actually like their commute. It gives them time to prepare for their day or wind down in the evening. They listen to audiobooks or their favorite music. They practice their favorite foreign language with tutorials. They use their hands-free phone aps to get some business calls done. Some people even take this opportunity to memorize scripture or engage in prayer time. I myself must abstain from prayer and worship for very long when in traffic. I tend to get caught up in these experiences and fail to concentrate on the road. This makes for an unbelievable explanation to the driver you just rear-ended, not to mention the nice state patrolman.

Then there are those traffic tie-ups that are unexplained. You're rolling along the highway on the way to some pleasant vacation destination in unknown territory. Then suddenly, WHAM! You're stuck in a traffic jam. You have no idea why everything has stopped. You turn on the local radio station, hoping for an update. More often than not, you hear multiple commercials, and then some program on how to prevent boll weevils. Rarely do you get a clue about the traffic incident. Of course there are stations that give you "five on the fives"—Five minutes of traffic and weather five minutes after the hour. Unfortunately, your traffic jam occurs at ten after, and you must wait 55 minutes for information. So you stick your head out of the window for a look. Invariably, the road bends ahead, and you can't see far enough to determine anything. If this goes on for very long, some of your fellow stuckees may get out of their cars and chat—speculating about the situation. Just pray you don't have several toddlers or teenagers with you when this happens. This multiplies your stress. And of course, you or at least one of your passengers, has an immediate bathroom emergency. The pressure is building. You have reservations. People are depending on you. You have no service on your cell phone!

What is a spiritual person to do? Are there any scriptures to assuage your trials at this moment?

Well, there are, but you may not be in the right frame of mind to receive the message. First you can know that God is in control. He knows your stress, He knows your needs. He is weaving together the lives of everyone stuck on the road. Trust Him and make the best of it. Romans 8:28 tells us that "we know that all things work together for good to them that love God, to them who are the called according to his purpose....." Besides, things are probably going much better for you than for the one who caused the traffic tie-up in the first place. Say a prayer for them, and distract the kids with music or games.

***

25

As bad as the traffic jam may seem, it's even worse to be stuck in your spiritual life. Have you reached a plateau? Do you feel like you've heard all the sermons before, prayed the same prayers, sung the same hymns? You're in a quagmire along with other Christians who seem complacent or insincere. What can you do?

It's easy to just sit in the pew, watching the world go by. Have you noticed that when someone points out a problem that they are then asked to be in charge of doing something about it. You don't want *that* to happen, do you? Well, do you? The answer is "yes!" The jam in your spiritual life isn't going away by itself. It might surprise you to see that all of the cars are stopped because you slowed down and blocked the lane. The best thing to do is remember who you are and why you are here. Jesus said that the greatest in the kingdom of heaven is a servant. A great way to "stir up the gift of God which is in you (2 Timothy. 1:6)...." is through service. Look at the mission or evangelism work that your church does. Ask God to show you the ministry where He can use your gifts.

In Paul's letter to the Ephesians, he encourages the Christians not to stop in their journey toward maturity as servants of Christ, but to grow. "Then we will no longer be infants, tossed back and forth by the waves, and blown here and there by every wind of teaching and by the cunning and craftiness of people in their deceitful scheming. Instead, speaking the truth in love, we will grow to become in every respect the mature body of him who is the head, that is, Christ. From him the whole body, joined and held together by every supporting ligament, grows and builds itself up in love, as each part does its work. (Ephesians. 4:14—16)

Or maybe it's outside your church. There are many organizations in your community that fulfill Jesus's challenge to feed the hungry, clothe the naked, help the weak. It won't take you long to find a place of service if you begin to look and pray. And don't hesitate to involve your children. Do you find that all the time-consuming activities you are frantically driving them to are centered on them? Encourage them to serve others as well. You will begin to stir up your spirit, and once you look out the window, you will notice the traffic jam is gone.

CHAPTER 8

Curves Ahead

My husband and I love to go to the North Georgia mountains for a get-away weekend. But whenever we go, there is a discussion about the driving route.

He: We can take the road over the mountain. It will be beautiful this time of year.

Me: You're right. It doesn't matter what time of year we go. In the winter there will be light layers of white snow on the banks of the mountain streams and frozen waterfalls emerging from the rocky cliffs.

He: And in the spring and summer, there are blooming trees and wild flowers. I guess the main decision is how fast do we want to get there?

Me: You're right. There's no quick route over the mountain. Just as soon as you build up to 35 miles an hour, you see one of those snaky road signs.

He: You mean "Curves Ahead."

Me: They even have those hairpin turns where you seem to be going back the way you just came! They make my ears pop and my stomach churn.

He: You're a wimp.

Me: I know. But you love me anyway.

He: Of course, we could just take the interstate and drive around the mountain and come out on the other side. We'd drive twice as many miles at less than half the time. There would be plenty of gas stations and fast food restaurants along the way. The radio reception is better and I can listen to talk radio all the way!

Me: That's right. We could, but let's not.

He: If we take the mountain road, it'll a lot longer. I'll have to turn off the radio. I don't even think I'll have cell reception up there.

My eyes brighten and I begin to smile.

He: You don't want to go interstate do you? If we go over the mountain, we'll just have to creep along. And you never know what will be around the next curve...

Me: Exactly!

***

As Christians, we are all busy, involved people. We are raising families, working full-time jobs, and attending church two or more nights a week. We serve on committees, visit the sick, attend community events, work in the house, and keep up our yards. We like to travel on nice straight roads without curves. We can get where we need to go quickly, without hitting the brakes. We have our lives precisely planned to the minute and wish that we could clone ourselves so that we could do even more of the same.

We're planning a trip on the interstate of life. Everyone is rapidly driving in the same direction. We don't have time for intersections where we meet up with other drivers. We can't really see what is outside the window—we're going too fast. The straightest route is the one we choose with no detours or rest stops if we can help it. If anyone in the back seat asks to stop for a break, we holler back, "Can't you hold it? I'm making good time here!"

"Curves Ahead" is a warning sign, but that doesn't have to be a bad thing. It's the curves on the road of life that bring us out of our brain fog and make us pay attention. Having a goal in mind is fine, but God throws us many curves that end up being much better than what we, in our short-sightedness, had so carefully planned.

Jesus told us to love our neighbors. When someone asked Him, "Who is my neighbor?" he told a parable about a man who was robbed and left to die on the road to Jericho. A Jewish priest came by, but was intent on getting to his appointment, so he passed by on the other side of the road. A Levite, or temple worker, did the same. But a Samaritan, who was a born enemy of the Jews, slowed down long enough to tend to the man and take him to safety. So the religious folks wouldn't help, but the enemy did.

"Which of these three do you think was a neighbor to the man who fell into the hands of robbers?" He asked. The expert in the law replied, "The one who had mercy on him." Jesus told him, "Go and do likewise." (Luke. 10:25)

You see, God wants us to be ready for something unexpected around the bend. He wants us to make the most of a situation, even if it interrupts our busy schedule. The best route in life isn't always a straight line!

It's like that winding road in the mountains. Just when you are asking yourself why you embarked on such a treacherous route, you reach the summit and a breathtaking vista opens up. You pull your car over and just inhale the beauty. Those curves will always be there to pull you out of your rut, even if it's a good rut. They will fill your life with unexpected encounters that will end up being the times you treasure most.

CHAPTER 9

Intersections — Part I

Decisions, Decisions

In the future, I think there should be roads with no intersections. In our electromagnetic cars with no wheels and no gas engines, we will program in our destination and slide along like the monorail at Disneyworld. It will be a beautifully choreographed dance with each person weaving in and out among the masses like a song. But, alas, this is not our fate at the moment. Once we leave the freeway, we must encounter each other at intersections.

Many interesting things happen at intersections. First we must slow down in anticipation of stopping or making a turn. This is another one of the times when your behavior is a direct result of what other drivers are doing. It would be fine if we were all going in the same direction, at the same speed. The truth is, however, that we are not.

What difference does it make how you approach an intersection? Is there a right way or a wrong way? A loving way or a self-serving way? A "love thy neighbor" way or an "every man for himself" way? You must know the answer by now.

There are many decisions to be made. Here is a nifty chart to illustrate some of them:

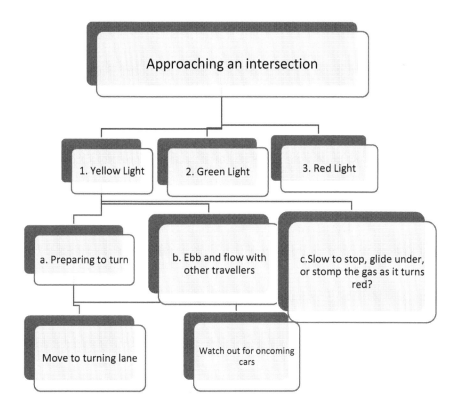

Take option 1—Yellow Light, slowing down. If you are planning to make a turn, it is kinder to check your mirrors for other drivers and move into the turning lane. This may require you to stop chatting on the phone and pay attention to where you are going. Why not even signal that you are moving over? That's a nice gesture for the mom one lane over who has been transporting her kids hither and thither all afternoon. Then she won't have to slam on the breaks when you zip into her lane at the last minute.

Your world of Christian influence includes your fellow drivers. A little bit of courtesy can be a blessing to the person one lane over.

Then there is option 1-b. Ebbing and flowing. As you all come to the light and it turns yellow, the guy in front of you slows slightly. You follow suit, as does the person in back of you whom you hope is not following too closely. This makes for a bit of a slow-down, but if everyone cooperates, it will pick right up. Slamming the brakes and laying on your horn because your neighbor is slowing usually doesn't speed things up at all. Cursing or throwing up digital hand signals does not set the best example for your kids. Take a breath and imagine that the road is a big ballroom, and the vehicles are the waltzing dancers. They ebb and flow—give and take-- as one couple twirls out and another takes their place. You're not really anxiously waiting for the dummy in front of you to get through the light before it turns red. No, you are generously allowing them to navigate towards their goal and waiting for your moment to do the same. It's a great time to remember the nature of Christian love—"Love is patient, love is kind…it is not easily angered." (I Corinthians. 13: 4-5)

Can you practice your Christian obedience while driving? I mean, who is going to know what's in your mind and heart when you are in your car where the other drivers can't see or hear you? Who will know if you are being gracious and patient with the other drivers or if you are smoldering and seething, muttering derogatory remarks? In Matthew chapter 6, Jesus tells us that your heavenly Father will see what you do in secret and will reward you. It will pay off down the road of life.

Option 1-c requires some thought. You're approaching an intersection and the light turns yellow. You could brake, but you're clipping along pretty well. You'd have to slam on the brakes and the guy behind you might run into you. It's really better to speed up, even though it might turn red. Right? It would really be better for everyone. Probably safer, too. Right? Unless, of course, there is one of those annoying traffic cameras trained on this intersection. Surely a nice judge would understand that you ran the light for the betterment of everyone. How should a Christian handle this common situation?

In a situation such as this, there are so many factors to consider in a split second. You have a responsibility to the law, but you are also considering your safety and the safety of others. You might call this a "gray area." And there is no time for prayer and meditation on the subject. So, you make your choice.

Let's say you push on through and the light turns red just as you shoot through the intersection. No biggie. No one was harmed. 'Nuff said. Then you hear it. "Whoop, whoop!" In your rearview mirror you see a police car flashing its lights. Man! What bad luck! Surely there are more serious crimes taking place at this moment. Why do they have to bother me?

Now it is time for more decisions. How will a Christian react to being pulled over? In this case, you really do deserve it, so it's not a question of whether you are guilty of disregarding the law. You must decide whether you will, argue, lie, or take your medicine. Should it depend on the attitude of the officer? Will that make a difference? Maybe you will know the officer! You know a lot of officers in this town. You could ask them for a break.

In Peter's first letter, he wrote to other Christians with these words: "Submit yourselves for the Lord's sake to every human authority: whether to the emperor, as the supreme authority, or to governors, who are sent by him to punish those who do wrong and to commend those who do right. For it is God's will that by doing good, you should silence the ignorant talk of foolish people. Live as free people, but do not use your freedom as a cover-up for evil; live as God's slaves." (1 Peter. 2:13-16)

Peter was no stranger to interactions with law enforcement. He openly preached the gospel when it was not allowed. He also was put in prison for it. But when counselling new Christians about obeying civil laws, he instructed them to abide by the laws and give respect to authority.

So when the officer asks for your license and registration, an obedient Christian would simply be respectful and comply. Reply honestly to questions and "take your medicine" if they give you a ticket. It's possible you will be warned. If so, be thankful and store that experience away for later. If nothing else, you will be a blessing to an officer who is usually scorned simply doing their job.

At a crossroad in life, when we make a snap decision, sometimes we get it right. Sometimes we don't. If there are consequences for a wrong decision, or even an honest mistake, God will be there to help us if we admit our sin and try to do better. "But if we confess our sins to him, he is faithful and just to forgive us our sins and to cleanse us from all wickedness." (1 John. 1:9)

CHAPTER 10

Intersections—Stop and Go

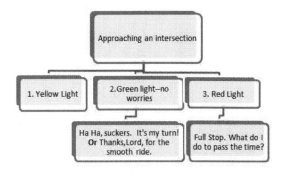

Have you had one of those days recently? Everything was just going great! You woke up feeling refreshed. No body aches or brain fog. The rest of the family was on point as well. The kids dressed themselves and didn't even fight over the bathroom. Your spouse left you plenty of hot water for your shower, and breakfast almost made itself. Your coffee was just the right temperature and your morning paper landed on the porch, not in the holly bush.

Now you're on your way. You drop the kids at school and you have just enough time to make it to work if traffic is not backed up. *And* if a train isn't stalled on the track. *And* if you don't get behind too many school buses. *And* if there is no road construction. *And* if there are no accidents on the highway. That's right. If all of the stars align, things will be fine. Yeah, right!

But even though it seems impossible, it all has happened just as you hoped. Just one more traffic light and you are home free! Could it be possible?

Yes! Yes, yes, yes! Just as you approach the intersection, you can tell that you are going to make it under the green light and sail on to your destination!

You begin this monologue in your head: "So long suckers, I'm movin' on down the road! I must be living right. No worries for me. Hey, there's a guy in the next lane trying to merge. You'll just have to wait for somebody who gives a hoot, cause I'm on a roll! Oh! There are some pedestrians waiting to cross to the park. You'll just have to 'park it' for a few more minutes, 'cause nothing will slow me down now.

There's the employee parking lot ahead. And old Grumpy Pants is heading for my favorite parking space. Nope! I got here first.

What? Don't I deserve one day all for myself? And I'm just beginning. This is going to be MY day, all the way!

Everyone deserves a perfect day once in a while. There's nothing wrong with that, but just because you are riding on a cloud, that's no reason to dump rain on everyone else. Even if you deserved your break, why not reach out and share the love? You ran through all of the green lights with time to spare, so whisper a prayer of thanks, and be generous with your fellow drivers. You can afford to let granny cross the road without breaking a hip.

***

So what is the spiritual equivalent of your perfect, green-light day? Some people mistakenly believe that once they accept Christ that He promises all sunshine and daffodils. Not so! The Christian should not expect things to go perfectly their way. But the good news is that however things go on the road of life, God is with you. He will give you His grace, His strength, and His joy to accompany you in fair and stormy weather. God has blessed you so that you may bless others.

In Paul's letter to Timothy, he tells us "Command those who are rich in this present world not to be arrogant nor to put their hope in wealth, which is so uncertain, but to put their hope in God, who richly provides us with everything for our enjoyment. Command them to do good, to be rich in good deeds, and to be generous and willing to share. In this way they will lay up treasure for themselves as a firm foundation for the coming age, so that they may take hold of the life that is truly life." (Timothy. 6:17-19) So when God blesses you in any way, use that opportunity to share your blessings with others on the road of life.

So that brings us to our last option when approaching an intersection. You can see that the signal is definitely red. That decision had been made for you. You must stop (or face the consequences). That means you have a moment to relax and take a breath. No merging, ebbing or flowing necessary. It's an easy time to be obedient. There's no way I can mess up this one.

Really? So have you ever heard someone uttering colorful language when "caught" by a red light? Of course you have. Get real. It happens every day. Things like "Man, it's not my day." "This light gets me every time." "I think there's a little troll in there that can see me coming." And much worse! In fact, you might be grumbling or whining so loudly that you miss the nice, little break you could be enjoying. Instead of stressing over the whole minute of drive time you added to your ride, take advantage of the time. Speak to your passengers--whisper a prayer for those at your destination or family members who are starting their day or whatever they are doing. Pray for your pastor, your boss, your church. Count your blessings. The options are countless. Just don't get so engrossed in your thoughts that you don't notice the light changing to green. Then that guy behind you will remind you that they are stressed too.

So does it really matter what I do while waiting at a stop light? What if I'm alone in my car? Who knows the difference? Take it a little further. Does is matter at all what I do when no one is looking? Or even if others are in the car with me? Can other drivers even see my expression, or do they notice my driving manners? Everyone gets irritated when driving, right?

Your behavior, and even your thoughts while driving, are a reflection of who you are as a whole. Working to please the Lord as you drive is a good way to practice for other situations that are sure to come your way as soon as you exit your vehicle. The scriptures tell us that he who is faithful in little will be faithful in much.

In Ephesians 4, Paul says, "Now this I say and testify in the Lord, that you must no longer walk as the Gentiles do, in the futility of their minds. They are darkened in their understanding, alienated from the life of God because of the ignorance that is in them, due to their hardness of heart. They have become callous and have given themselves up to sensuality, greedy to practice every kind of impurity. But that is not the way you learned Christ!-- assuming that you have heard about him and were taught in him, as the truth is in Jesus, to put off your old self, which belongs to your former manner of life and is corrupt through deceitful desires, and to be renewed in the spirit of your minds, and to put on the new self, created after the likeness of God in true righteousness and holiness."

As we have seen, your driving life is a microcosm of your spiritual walk. If you practice faithfulness behind the wheel, you will have some righteous experience under your belt for your next challenge. Keep that in mind the next time the red light catches you.

CHAPTER 11

Sightseeing

As we drive along a new stretch of road, it's fun to notice the new things we see along the way. A long road trip can get tedious, so making observations about the people and things we see out the window can help pass the time. While the driver needs to focus on the traffic and road signs, passengers can enjoy the scenery, the buildings, and the people going by.

The car enthusiasts enjoy viewing the wide range of cars, trucks, and motorcycles in endless parade. They notice the makes, models, and special modifications in great detail. They can quote the engine specifications and can even identify a car just by its sound.

Others in the car might only tell one car from another by the color. They are more interested in the people inside the cars. They notice the clothing and hairstyles of the pedestrians or speculate about the relationships between the people at the bus stop. These are the people-watchers, and they can entertain themselves during the urban traffic crawl just by taking in the colorful mix of the crowd.

My husband is a nature guy. He loves to take in the flora and fauna of any new place we go. He notices the genre of every tree along the roadside and can spot a hawk on a branch hundreds of yards away. With his background in wildlife management, he appreciates the beauty of a swamp and the grandeur of the foothills in the distance. He has his field guides handy just in case we take a stretch break at a forest byway.

Others in the group are the tour guides. They are on the lookout for great places to eat or drink, and fun things for everyone to do. They want to get out of the car at regular intervals to make the most of the culture of the places along the route. A trip without fun along the way is not worth taking.

Each person on your road trip sees a different way to make the most of the experience. Seeing the world through the eyes of others helps us understand all of the blessings that can be enjoyed. Although getting to your destination is important, so much can be achieved by sharing the experience with others.

***

Just as we can appreciate the viewpoint of our fellow travelers, God blesses each spirit-filled Christian with special gifts that are meant to be shared with the body. These gifts are named in several places in the scriptures. In Ephesians 4, it mentions gifts that are useful for the work of service in the church. "So Christ himself gave the apostles, the prophets, the evangelists, the pastors and teachers, to equip his people for works of service, so that the body of Christ may be built up." (Ephesians. 4:11-12) These reach out to other Christians with wisdom and encouragement from The Holy Spirit to serve as leaders in the church. In Romans 12, the scripture says to actively use your gift freely, liberally and happily. As you share the strengths you have, also look for gifts in other Christians and encourage them to practice them.

Some have healing gifts, some can discern the needs and gifts of others, and some can communicate closely with God. No one manifests all of the gifts. Instead, God wants each of us to depend on the other and work together to know Him, to worship Him, and to tell others about Him. God made us to be creatures who need each other and who need to give to each other. As the world sees us in unity with The Spirit, they can see our love for each other. They will want to know how it is possible. It is then that they will listen as we tell them about the joy of knowing Christ.

On the cornerstone of my church, there is an inscription that is the motto of our congregation—"Loving one another to Christ." This is what Jesus meant when he spoke about the glorious day when we would stand before His throne, and he would welcome the acceptable ones into His Kingdom.

"Come, you who are blessed of My Father inherit the kingdom prepared for you from the foundation of the world. For I was hungry, and you gave Me something to eat; I was thirsty, and you gave Me drink; I was a stranger, and you took me in; naked, and you clothed Me. I was sick, and you visited Me, I was in prison, and you came to Me." (Matthew. 25:35)

When the righteous didn't remember doing this for Jesus, He told them that if they did it for any person, even the one who was considered the lowliest and least, it was the same as doing it for Him.

So, know that God has given you a gift--something special that you can do for His kingdom. If you haven't discovered it yet, pray, asking God to reveal it to you. Ask those on the journey with you to help you find it. Once you discover your gift and share it with others, you will make the journey more satisfying for all those around you.

CHAPTER 12

Struggling Up the Hill

Disclaimer: This trip actually took place. The names have not been changed, but some of the details may have been embellished.

On one of our frequent trips to the mountains, my family made their way north to the rolling hills of Tennessee. Cruising down the interstate brought us into the Volunteer State, and the going was easy. Every time we topped a hill, there was one more waiting—just a little higher. We exited the main road and took to the winding two-lanes. Our goal was the vacation cabin of a dear family friend who had loaned us the use of their get-away home for a week.

It was quite a group: Me and the Hubs (Chip), our kids Josh and Megan, their two friends Walter and Sydney, Chip's brothers Curtis and

Chris, and Mother Cox. With such a large crowd and plans to go in different directions during the week, we decided to take two vehicles—our full-sized van and Curtis's smaller sedan. We had planned to stay in touch on the drive by chatting back and forth with the use of walkie- talkies.

Off-roads in the hill country are not always clearly marked, but we managed to find our way. Small farms hugged the mountainsides with lots of random farm vehicles, barns and siloes accenting the fields and pastures. Suddenly, we saw the road sign we were looking for. There didn't seem to be any cabin-like structures around. And then we looked up. And up. And up. Hanging off a cliff about a half-mile up the mountain, we saw a cabin. At first it wasn't clear how a vehicle could get up there. I wondered if we were going to have to unload here in the valley and pack our belongings up on our backs like Tibetan sherpas.

Then I could see that there actually was a "road" zig-zagging up the incline. Not a paved road, but one of dirt and gravel. The slope was so steep, even with the switchbacks, that I honestly thought there was no way our van-full of family, gear, and supplies could possibly make it to the top.

"Too bad we don't have four-wheel-drive," I muttered. "No problem!" chirped my hubby.

"Mom, you're not going to let him drive up that pig trail, are you!?" asked Megan cautiously.

"Are we there yet?" piped Josh, with his headphones on, playing a video game and oblivious to the situation at hand.

"Breaker, breaker, this is Ranger, come on?" Chip spoke into the walkie.

"This is Ultraman, reading you loud and clear," squawked Curtis in answer.

"Uh, you got this?" questioned Chris, looking skeptically at the narrow trail.

"That's a big 10-4" answered back his big brother.

"Maybe you'd better take the lead. If you start to slide, I'll be your safety net," said Curtis.

"Safety net? Slide? Is your dad crazy?" whispered Sydney to her best friend.

"You're not serious, are you, Dad?" said Megan. "I know I saw a motel a few miles back. There's no shame in admitting defeat!"

"Now, sweetie, don't you have faith in your good old dad? I'm a game and fish ranger, for goodness sakes. A little hill won't give me any trouble."

"Hey, Dad," Josh piped in. "Do you think they'll have satellite tv up there? I think this looks like the highest point around."

"Uh, honey, I think that the kids and I will just get out and look at the local wild flowers for a few minutes. Stretch our legs, you know. You can drive up and start unloading, and we'll just walk up for some exercise after our long drive," I suggested.

"Now, wait a minute. You don't actually have faith that I will make it up there, do you?" sneered my husband.

"It's not that, dear, it's just…"

"Okay, Ranger," squawked the walkie –talkie, "This is Ultraman, taking the point."

And with that, Curtis spun his tires and zoomed around our van, spraying gravel in his wake.

The little sedan started up the slope with its back end swaying slightly as the tires dug into the rocky ruts.

"Here we go!" Chip shouted out the window, and our van followed behind—leaving a generous gap for flying rocks and dirt.

Megan and Sydney gripped each others' hands as they stared ahead with expressions of anxiety. "I'm so sorry…I had no idea it would be like this," I heard Megan whisper.

Josh and Walter grinned at the girls. "If we slide off the mountain, they probably won't find our bodies for days," Josh said merrily as Walter snickered.

"That's not very helpful, Josh," I said through gritted teeth. "Oh, watch out, Honey! You're too close to the edge!"

Up ahead, the in-law car had reached the first switch-back. "How's it going back there, Ranger?" squawked the walkie. "Are you eating my dust yet?"

"He's not getting away with that," growled Chip. "Sweetie, hold that walkie-talkie over here by me. I've got a great comeback for that one."

"Never mind that. Just keep your eyes on the road," I said shakily. I watched as our lead car shimmied on up the slope at a steady clip. As we completed the zig and approached the acute angle switch to zag, I called upon the limited geometric knowledge in my distant past. "Honey, I don't think it's mathematically possible for this van to navigate that turn."

"Have a little faith, Sweetie. Have a little faith." The Hubs punched the gas, masterfully turned the wheel, and guided the boxy, heavy van around the bend and on up the trail.

I looked at the face of the man who had led our family through so many ups and downs of life. There was not a trace of doubt in his expression. In fact, the challenge before him had energized him. Instead of a reckless kid trying to show his little brother a thing or two, I saw a man who would never put the family he loves in jeopardy no matter how he was goaded. He was ready for the trials of the road ahead and determined to bring us all to our goal.

"You're right, Honey," I agreed. "Hold on kids, we're gonna have a great vacation or die trying!"

"Go, Dad! Go, Dad! Go Dad!" the kids chanted from the back. The van moved onward and upwards—zigging and zagging—and soon we reached the summit. Waiting by the sedan were my two brothers-in-law, leaning smugly against the car, arms folded. My mother-in-law was climbing out of the back seat looking rather pale.

As we exited the van and began to allow our tightly clasped limbs to unwind, the brothers piped up.

"What took you so long, Chip?" piped Chris.

"Yeah, we already unloaded the car and grabbed up a load of fire wood waiting for you to get here," said Curtis.

Chip just grinned. "I was just taking my time, pointing out the scenery to the kids. Since you've had some time to rest, you can unload our car, too. I'm ready to jump in the hot tub." And with that, he skipped up the cabin steps, unlocked the door and disappeared inside.

"You don't think he was serious, do you?" asked Chris.

As the kids ran down to the creek, I grinned. "What do you think, Mother Cox?" I asked with a smile.

"I think it would be better for everyone if you two did what your big brother asked," she said wisely.

The two younger brothers took a moment and looked at each other. Then they trudged over to the van, and began unloading the gear.

***

On the road of life, each of us encounters challenges. It is fascinating to see how each person faces these situations. Our trip up the mountain reminds me of the time when Jesus was on the Sea of Galilee with the disciples. He was sleeping when a storm began to brew. "The disciples went and woke him, saying, 'Lord, save us! We're going to drown!' He replied, 'You of little faith, why are you so afraid?' Then he got up and rebuked the winds and the waves, and it was completely calm." (Matthew. 8:26)

On our trip, Chip got it right. He looked at the difficulty before him and knew that he had the strength and skill to overcome it. Eventually I saw through my fears and began to have faith in my partner, who had seen our family through many troubled times.

When struggling up the hills in your life, don't forget that the master of the storm is in the boat with you. He will calm the storms around you and within you.

CHAPTER 13

Maintenance

Everyone remembers the day you got your first car. Maybe it was a gift from your parents on the day you passed the driver's test. It might have been out in the driveway on a Christmas morning. Or perhaps you saved up your paychecks until you had enough for a down payment. Whether it was a gift or earned with lots of sweat equity, it felt so great to get behind the wheel and take it out for that first drive.

When the car comes off the lot, it is in pristine condition with that "new car" smell. Even a previously-owned car has passed all of the safety checks and is clean and sharp. Mom and Dad are sure to instruct you on the way to maintain your vehicle to keep it in the best condition. Car ownership is a privilege, and if you care for it properly from the beginning, you will be safe and comfortable.

The proper maintenance is also a responsibility. Laws are in place to insure that your headlights and turn signals can be seen clearly by other drivers. Tires should be inflated properly and kept in proper alignment so that no mishaps will cause an accident, harming you or your fellow drivers. Brakes must be checked on a regular basis along with oil changes. So many parts work together to keep your vehicle ready to get you to your destination safely.

So how does maintenance relate to your Christian witness? What effect does it have on those around you? Well, first think about the passengers in your car--family, friends, colleagues, or neighbors. Keeping a clean car shows that you are thankful for your blessings, and it makes the ride more welcoming and pleasant for them. God has given you the means to buy your own vehicle, and that's a blessing. As with all blessings, if you give your car to God, He will give you opportunities to use it for Him. When you look for Him in everyday experiences, He will take whatever you offer—whether it be time, money or belongings—and give you a chance to bless others in return. Maybe there is someone who isn't able to drive who needs a ride to church. Or maybe someone needs a ride home—giving you some quiet time to talk and establish a friendship. God will surprise you if you give Him a chance.

Keeping your car in good driving condition makes you a safer driver, and that transfers to other drivers on the road. If you fail to check up on your brakes, turn signals, belts, and fluids, you are just an accident waiting to happen—putting yourself and others on the road at risk. So next time you pull in for an oil change and tire rotation, remember that you are not just doing something for yourself, but you are blessing others by making the road a safer place!

***

Good car maintenance depends on the reliability of each part of the vehicle. Remember the old spiritual "Dem Bones"? The head bone's connected to the neck bone. The neck bone's connected to the shoulder bone. Etc. It's the same thing with your car. The ignition connects to the battery that sends juice to the starter that cranks the engine. Spark plugs fire the gas that is sent by the fuel pump to the engine and sprayed into the engine by means of the fuel injectors. Once the engine is running, it is attached to the transmission and the crankshaft spins the shaft going to the rear wheels. The rear axle causes the side axle shafts to spin and away you go! But if just one part in the sequence fails to function, the car doesn't go.

In 1 Corinthians 12, Paul reminds us that the body of Christ works in a similar way. "There is one body, but it has many parts. But all its many parts make up one body. It is the same with Christ. We were all baptized by one Holy Spirit. And so we are formed into one body. It didn't matter whether we were Jews or Gentiles, slaves or free people. We were all given the same Spirit to drink. So the body is not made up of just one part. It has many parts.

Suppose the foot says, "I am not a hand. So I don't belong to the body." By saying this, it cannot stop being part of the body. And suppose the ear says, "I am not an eye. So I don't belong to the body." By saying this, it cannot stop being part of the body. If the whole body were an eye, how could it hear? If the whole body were an ear, how could it smell? God has placed each part in the body just as he wanted it to be. If all the parts were the same, how could there be a body? As it is, there are many parts. But there is only one body...

But God has put together all the parts of the body. And he has given more honor to the parts that didn't have any. In that way, the parts of the body will not take sides. All of them will take care of one another. If one part suffers, every part suffers with it. If one part is honored, every part shares in its joy. You are the body of Christ. Each one of you is a part of it."

As you continue on your life journey, remember that you are an important part of the body of Christ and of His mission in the world. You may be a real spark plug of a person—one who can easily share God's word with other people. Or you may be an encourager—giving much-needed fuel to people who are discouraged. Maybe you are the distributer cap--an organizer who helps plan the mission work of your church. Or maybe you are one of those rare people who can help people see where the rubber meets the road—telling them the truth they that really need to hear.

The church needs all of the parts to keep working for its job to be done. Make sure your spiritual maintenance chart is up to date so that you are ready to do what God wants from you. Stay connected to fellow Christians and stay in touch with God through prayers and time in His word. Then you are doing your part to keep the body in good working order under the loving eye of the Master Mechanic.

CHAPTER 14

Parking Lots

Parking is actually just another act of driving. In fact, a parking lot is a microcosm of the larger dynamics experienced on the road. There are rules here, people! But do the laws that we are normally required to abide by apply to parking lots? On the road, we are operating on government property, but many parking lots are considered private property. So if official laws don't always apply, what about common courtesy? What about basic safety concerns? Do we just leave them at the curb? In the end, we all are just looking for a place to park, right?

First let's consider the drivers entering the parking lot. They are making the transition from travelling to settling. They have reached their destination, and now they are ready to stop for a while and engage in some anticipated activity. They would like to find a convenient parking spot with little fuss involved.

Most parking lots have some sort of directional markings showing the drivers the layout of the desired traffic flow. Many lanes are one-way. Some lots have angled parking spaces while others are straight-on, allowing for parking on either side of the lane. Most markings are bold and easily understood, making the slow, careful traffic flow easy for any observant driver. Right?

Oh no, my friend. It's not that simple.

Be honest. A savvy driver must be as much on guard in a busy parking area as he is on the road. Yes, there are arrows indicating the direction that traffic should flow, but many people see those as mere suggestions, not hard and fast laws. It's just a parking lot, so all bets are off. There are no officers ready to pull you over if you don't abide by the rules. So here are some of the parking lot rule-benders you may meet in a typical parking lot.

The cross-country parkers. The cross-country parkers totally ignore that there are parking spaces or lanes indicated. They take off across the black-top headed for the spot of their choice as if it were an open prairie. Other drivers had better get out of the way. In fact, they are highly annoyed by those of us who carefully maneuver in and out of the indicated lanes as if **we** are the ones behaving outside the norm. **Your best option:** Just hope that they see you and will avoid hitting you, since that would just slow them down. When encountering a cross-country parker, it is best to just stop and let them go by. There is no way to read their minds.

The clueless parkers. These precious souls are very focused, but their focus is not on their driving. They are focused on whatever is going on in their own little worlds. It may be the brilliant conversation they are having on their cell phone. It may be the fact that they are waiting for a particular space to be vacated, and no other spot will do. They will sit there blocking the lane for as long as it takes. They see that the owner of the car currently occupying the space is loading up their car with recently-purchased items and will be leaving sometime in the next half-hour. Or maybe they are just waiting for someone inside the store.

Your best option: In most cases, no amount of polite honking will convince them to move along. If you are lucky, you might be able to get their attention by yelling out the window. A good Christian response would be to assume that they don't realize that their behavior is deliberately rude. A simple "Hello, I'd like to get by" might get the best results. Rage and cursing is most likely to entrench them in their spot.

The catty-wompus parkers. There are several sub-categories of catty-wompus parkers. Some deliberately park in such a way as to take up at least two parking spaces. Their vehicles are evidently so valuable that there should be no chance that another car might get near them. Others are either young, inexperienced drivers or older drivers who can no longer see the lines. They have good intentions, but they can't seem to get it right. Then there are just good folks who have so much on their minds that they don't even notice their parking faux pas. They are so close to the line that no one could park next to them and have room to open their door.

Your best option: Choose a spot some distance away. They are likely to have as much trouble exiting their space as they did when they pulled in, and you might be the recipient of their bad driving.

Pedistrians. Not only must you contend with the drivers in a parking lot, but there are the pedestrians making their way to and from the venue. Your mother surely taught you to walk along next to the cars and not in the middle of the driving lane. You know that you should be alert, noticing whether drivers are about to back up and staying in view for your safety and theirs. So who raised the people to stroll leisurely right down the middle of the lane, chatting on their phones or to another clueless lane-hogger?

It's hard to swallow your frustration and creep along until they notice the five cars backed up behind them.

Your best option: No, you can't just mow them down for their offenses. That's not Christian. Sometimes I find that giving them clever names and a back story helps to diffuse my anger. So let's just call them Horace and

Doris who only get to town once a year to buy groceries and are savoring every moment of the experience by slowly lollygagging down the lane.

Finally you manage to park, making sure you are entrenched evenly between the lines. You let go of the stress of the parking lot blues, and you find that--just as with the pain of childbirth—the angst is quickly forgotten, and you can go about your business.

***

Jesus didn't have to weather the storms of parking lot driving, but He certainly encountered large, unpredictable crowds of people. He didn't stay in an ivory tower, waiting for the needy souls to come to Him. He went out to meet them where they lived--at work manning the fishing nets by the sea, in the marketplaces, on the streets of the towns, in their homes, and at their worship. It was not neat and orderly, and not everyone was playing by the rules. He did not shy away from the scholars who opposed Him, but engaged them in spirited dialogue, answering the questions they didn't even know they were asking.

And at another time He heard the unspoken cry of an elderly woman suffering from debilitating illness—a woman who would have been shunned and ignored in her culture. Not only did he notice her, but he showed her mercy and respect.

"She came up behind him and touched the edge of his cloak, and immediately her bleeding stopped. "Who touched me?" Jesus asked. When they all denied it, Peter said, "Master, the people are crowding and pressing against you." But Jesus said, "Someone touched me; I know that power has gone out from me." Then the woman, seeing that she could not go unnoticed, came trembling and fell at his feet. In the presence of all the people, she told why she had touched him and how she had been instantly healed. Then he said to her, "Daughter, your faith has healed you. Go in peace." (Luke. 4:43-48)

The parking lot of life is where we encounter the rebels, the clueless, and the ones who have gone sideways. Instead of seeing them as annoyances, see them as Christ did—as souls in need, who would be joyfully surprised by an unexpected response from fellow drivers who have pulled off the road for a moment. Maybe in that moment, you can breathe a prayer and hear a message from God that they need to hear. If given the chance, deliver the message. Not only will it surprise them, it will surprise you what God will do if you are willing to hear Him.

CHAPTER 15

Fender Benders

With so many people driving so erratically in so many directions with so much on their minds, it is inevitable that every now and then, they will bump into each other. Unfortunately, many such accidents can result in serious injury to the drivers and cause irreparable damage to the vehicles. But there are also what we refer to as "fender benders." These are the more minor incidents where little injury occurs to the drivers, and there is just enough damage to the car to be irritating and inconvenient.

A few months ago I was at the hairdresser's salon getting a refresher to my highlights and lowlights. This takes some time and involves the stylist painting locks of hair with various colors and rolling it up in aluminum foil. As the process advances, I begin to look like something out of a science fiction novel with me wrapped up in a black cape with silver spikes sticking out of my head. A person feels quite vulnerable at this point, and it is an unwritten rule that women don't take pictures in a salon so as not to take advantage of a fellow female in such an unflattering situation.

Just when I was looking my worst, the receptionist came up to my chair and said, "Mrs. Cox, do you drive a red Kia?" I was instantly worried that I had left off the parking break, and that my car had rolled down the hill and into some other car.

"Yes, I do. How did you know?"

"There is a gentleman at the front desk asking about it. I'm sorry to say that there has been an accident."

I glanced in the mirror and could not decide what horrified me more— the thought that my car was in an accident, or the thought that I was going to have to go out in public in my current state of headdress. I looked across the room to see a nice young man standing awkwardly by the counter, waving to me. I asked my stylist if it would impede the coloring process if I were to leave the salon for a few minutes. She informed me that it would not, and I could see the sympathy she had for my uncomfortable predicament.

I grabbed my purse and walked towards the man. We introduced ourselves as he began to explain what had happened. He had just gotten a haircut and was leaving the salon to go pick up his daughter at daycare. The lot was full, and he misjudged the distance between cars as he backed up. He hit my back right quarter panel with the bumper of his car. As he was speaking, we arrived at my car. I could see that he had pulled his vehicle back into his parking space. He pointed to the back of my car. At first glance, the damage did not look too bad. There was a small scratch and dent. Then as I looked more closely, I could see that some plastic trim had broken.

I wasn't feeling anger so much as irritation. First, over the damage, and also over my ridiculous state of dress.

"I don't think it's very serious," the man was saying. "I guess I was in a hurry to go get my daughter."

As a mom, I was instantly concerned that a call to the police and subsequent waiting would strand his little girl at the daycare. I was also quite concerned as to what would happen to my hair if I stayed too long in the parking lot with the chemicals on my head.

"I work for a body shop," he said. "What would you say if I spoke to my manager and just offered to fix the damage without involving a police or insurance report?"

Now I'm usually a stickler for obeying rules, but under the circumstance, I was anxious to get back to the stylist's chair. I had a gut feeling that the man was sincere, and that it probably wasn't necessary to make a formal report.

"All right. Let's exchange information," I said. We exchanged business cards, license numbers, looked at each other's driver's licenses and agreed that he would call me after his boss assessed the damage. All the while, I was wondering if I was making a big mistake. Maybe the chemicals had gone to my brain! I went back inside and finished my appointment without any more ado.

A few days after I had taken my car for the damage assessment, I received a call from the nice young man.

"Mrs. Cox," he said hesitantly, "I think we are going to have to go through the insurance company after all. The damage was more than we thought."

This is not what I wanted to hear. I was mentally kicking myself for giving the guy the benefit of the doubt. Maybe I had made a mistake about calling the police. "Okay. Have your insurance adjustor call me," I said reluctantly.

Sometimes I feel like I am too big of a pushover. I began to chastise myself. "Of course there was more damage. This guy probably can't pay for it, either. What a dummy, you are, Terri. On the other hand, the guy didn't have to seek you out at the salon that day. He could have just driven off without saying a word. Sometimes you just have to listen to you heart and do what it tells you."

The next day, the adjustor came by my office and said that he would like to look at my car. He went out to the parking lot and took pictures, made measurements and then went to his car for some phone calls. After a while, he called me out there and offered me a check for more than the repair estimate. I was pleasantly surprised. I had managed to avoid disaster on this one.

So what is the lesson to be learned from the fender bender? Did I behave as a good Christian? If a person bumps into you on the right rear panel, do you turn the other bumper? Or would I have set a better example if I had followed the letter of the law?

I don't think it really mattered in this case whether I gave the fellow the benefit of the doubt or if I had just followed the rules. Neither was morally wrong. What matters when you face a fender bender is not how you respond to the bump, but how you treat the people involved.

Here was a man whom I had never met. I'll probably never meet him again. Who knows? But in that moment of conflict, we each had the opportunity to show kindness to one another. We never did get the chance to share about the Lord. But as I mentioned before, he did go out of his way to find me and take responsibility for his mistake. I did show compassion for his daughter by making sure her father showed up for her on time. I showed faith in him and his effort to make sure my car was fixed. Then we went on our separate ways. It is the people that matter, not the possessions we own.

***

In our everyday lives, there will be accidents and fender benders—troubles and things that go wrong. In fact, at my job, I sometimes refer to each day as "a little pile of problems." Difficulties are to be expected, and no one is exempt. Christ says "in this world you <u>will</u> have trouble, but take heart! I have overcome the world."(John. 16:33)

When you experience these everyday problems-- be they great or small-- remind yourself that these are the times when we have the biggest influence on others. If someone wants to know how a professed Christian handles real life, they are now tuned in and ready to see if you really believe what you say. Does being a Christian make a difference in your life? Does it give you strength and wisdom, kindness and understanding, or will you react to trouble just like everyone else? To take it even further, be thankful for the troubles. They give you a chance to share your Christian witness.

At the start of your drive each day, it would open up a whole new opportunity for you if you would pray this prayer: Dear God, whatever trouble comes my way today, let your Spirit guide my words and my reactions. Give me a chance to share your love in any troublesome situation.

Give it a try. You might be pleasantly surprised with the results.

CHAPTER 16

Speed Limits

Speed limits are guidelines for drivers designed for optimum safety in a particular location. On the highway there are minimum and maximum speed limits. I remember my driver's education teacher from high school saying that the most dangerous car on the highway is a stopped car. And it's true. With hundreds of cars racing along at high speeds, the most serious accidents happen when someone stops suddenly. When a speeding object impacts an object at rest, the laws of physics can take over in an instant. Mass, velocity and inertia take the control out of our hands, and these tons of modern technology become dangerous monsters. The limits may seem like a nuisance at times, but they are there for our safety.

Most of us don't take the speed limit that seriously. We take note of the posted limit, but generally go over it to some degree, hoping not to get caught. We try to run with the pack, knowing that they can't catch all of us. We believe that we know our own driving skills and what is safe for us. Many times on the interstate I find myself in a wave of traffic all going well over the limit. If I maintain the posted speed, I feel that I will be in danger. If I stay at the limit, other cars begin passing on both sides. They honk and swerve and, though I can't hear them, I can just imagine the unsavory words they are saying. What's a Christian driver to do?

On the flip side, there are the speed traps. Those small communities along the highway where they intentionally set their speed limits quite a bit lower than surrounding areas in order to rack up speeding fines. I know of several in my area, and make sure to mind my P's and Q's when passing through. But do I get credit for obeying the law only because I know I am likely to get caught if I don't?

You can tell a lot about a person by their body language—facial expressions, eye contact, positions of the hands and arms, posture and other clues. It's also somewhat true with driving behavior. You can make fairly accurate assumptions about other drivers from their driving method of operation or m.o. You can tell a lot about someone by how they react to speed limits.

So one day I was on my morning commute. I had all of the speed zones memorized and could vary my speed appropriately without even thinking about it. There were several long, winding stretches where the speed limit is 45 mph and there were no places for passing. I noticed a fairly new red sports car approaching me from behind. I could tell by his driving m.o. that the driver was not going to be content to poke along behind me. He pulled within a few feet of my bumper and stayed there, encouraging me to "speed it up." Then he weaved over the center line a time or two, trying to see if he could get away with passing me, but the sight lines just wouldn't permit it.

I could have sped up a bit, but it amused me to see his frustration. Then, in a burst of bravado, he stomped the gas, pulled out and zoomed around me. Luckily he avoided a collision with an oncoming car with room to spare. Then two minutes down the road, I pulled up beside him, as he was stopped at a traffic light. I couldn't help flashing him a big grin. After taking such a big risk, he wasn't one bit further down the road than I was. Was I wrong to enjoy the intense feeling of vindication?

We often believe that we know what limits to place on our lives and that we don't really need God's limits. Just like many drivers, we don't take the limits seriously. We think of God's laws as His way of controlling us or spoiling our fun. We like driving or living outside the posted limits. It gives us a feeling of freedom and power. We forget that the limits are there to keep us safe—to lead us to the best outcomes possible. We must remember that God sees the road ahead. Not just for the individual, but for all of those on the road around us.

Have you ever been speeding along and come upon a slowpoke, driving two miles under the limit. You get stuck there for what seems like forever. A little further down the road, you encounter a terrible accident. You think to yourself, "Man! If I hadn't had to slow down, that could have been me!" It may be a cliché, but that pokey person may have been your guardian angel.

A spiritually-minded friend of mine in college would often drive the van for our musical group. He would pray, asking God for His protection before a trip. He was always tempted to go over the speed limit, but tried very hard to resist the temptation. He said that he would picture our guardian angel flying above the van with a big umbrella of protection. The angel was set to fly no faster than the posted speed limit. If he drove too fast, he would be taking us outside of God's protection. In other words, as long as we are obedient, God's protection would cover us. If we chose to move outside of the law, we were out on our own, so to speak.

Let's be honest. Speed limits are hard to obey. Human nature causes us to think we can figure out what is best for us at any given time. Some person decided what my limits should be, but do they really know my situation? I'll do what seems right to me. Or maybe I will abide by them most of the time, but just not right now. Humans are really good at rationalizing why giving in to temptation is really okay at certain times. You didn't know that driving over the limit was such a deep subject, did you?

***

As a Christian, you are given the scriptures to guide you—your speed limits. The Bible tells us to obey the laws of man as long as they do not conflict with God's laws. Your dilemma over keeping the speed limit is not an uncommon problem. So why do we need to obey the law—even when no one is watching? In the scriptures we are told that obeying the law is basically showing love. That's right. Think of any traffic law. The speed limit, for example. When we stay within the limits, we are keeping our fellow travelers safer (as well as ourselves).

Romans 13:9 says, "For the commandments, "You shall not commit adultery, You shall not murder, You shall not steal, You shall not covet," **and any other commandment**, are summed up in this word: "You shall love your neighbor as yourself."

The Christian life could be viewed as a life of constant limits. Do this, don't do that. But that's not what God intended. Once Christ paid the price for our sin, He set us free. Free to hear the voice of The Holy Spirit guiding us, without having to memorize the rulebook. He will show you what is right. You are free to choose it and live a life of joy and blessing. Or choose to ignore His urging and head towards the desert. It's your choice.

We cannot completely see the big picture in life. If God has given us commandments, rules, limits—whatever you choose to call them—then they are there to guide us towards what is best for all of us. Once you begin to drive under His umbrella, you will begin to reap the blessings He has planned for you.

CHAPTER 17

Directions

Every driver needs to get directions from time to time. Modern technology has changed this experience tremendously. Today we can use our smart phones or GPS navigation devices to get accurate routes to just about anywhere. There are times, however, when technology fails and we must revert to the old-school methods of finding the way. The most commons reasons for needing directions are going somewhere you have not been before or getting lost and needing help to get back on the correct path.

It is cliché to say that men will do just about anything to avoid stopping for directions (even though most clichés are based partially in fact.) So I'll just say that "some people" are hard-wired to go by their instincts rather than admit that they are lost. And one of those people was my Daddy.

One famous story in my family involved a trip to Athens, Georgia to attend a University of Georgia football game. My father was a proud bulldog alumnus, as were many other members of my family. We currently lived about two hours from UGA, and there was no easy route from here to there. Going from memory, Daddy took off down the winding two-lane roads of north Georgia in the general direction of Athens. At first my mom, my sister Paula, my five-year-old brother Andrew, and I were excited about the trip. My sister was planning to attend UGA the next year, and we all were looking forward to touring the campus and getting to see the mascot Uga, the bulldog, in person. It was a beautiful fall north Georgia day, and the leaves were in full color. After an hour or so, we began to anticipate seeing the road signs telling us that Athens was not far away. But then Mom began to express some questions about our location.

"Paul, I don't remember ever coming this way before," she said.

"It's a shortcut. I know exactly where I am," Daddy replied.

Now my dad was a very wise and determined fellow, having survived childhood polio and never expecting any special treatment for his disabilities. He came from a working-class family with little money to spare, but lots of faith in God and a big, close extended family. He put himself through University of Georgia journalism school and went from paper boy to publisher during the span of his career. No one liked to correct my Daddy, including my Mom.

After another little while, I became worried and piped in, "Daddy, there's a service station. Why don't you stop for directions?" Everyone got quiet for a moment, wondering how Daddy would take this.

"I don't need any gas," he replied. I guess that was my answer.

The silence became heavier and heavier as the road ahead got narrower and more deserted. The trees along the roadside seemed to get closer, and the houses and farmsteads farther apart. No one really knew what to say. And then the paved road came to an end and was replaced by gravel and dirt.

"Daddy?" said my sister, Paula.

"What," Daddy said through gritted teeth.

"Nothing," she wisely replied.

Finally Daddy braked and stopped the car. This was no concern about us blocking the road since we had not seen another car for quite some time.

We all sat there in silence for a moment. Now Andrew, being five years old, had not picked up on the tension of the situation. He was to get the message that we were lost.

"Daddy?" he chimed in.

"Yes, son," Daddy said.

"Are we lost?"

We all held our breath, waiting for Daddy's reply.

"'Cause if we are," Andrew continued, "you could just get out and climb a tree. Then you could see how to get us there," he merrily advised.

Then we all lost it! The whole family began to laugh.

"That's a good idea, son," Daddy said. "Why didn't I think of that?"

"Because I have a fresh young brain, Daddy," he replied matter-of-factly.

"I guess that's right, you do," Daddy said as a grin beamed across his face, "but I think I'll just turn around and go back to that service station and ask for directions."

We made it to Athens a little later than planned, but in plenty of time to see the Bulldogs playing between the hedges and Uga trotting down the sidelines. I don't remember precisely, but I'm sure the bulldogs won that day, and the Miles family had an experience we would never forget.

***

Jesus told several parables about being lost. In Luke 15, we hear the story of the prodigal son. He was anxious to begin his journey on the road of life, so he took his inheritance and left home. He squandered his money on fast living and lost his way. He was too embarrassed to go back home to the father who knew the right direction, so he took up with a stranger who gave him a job feeding swine. For a Jew, this was a degrading path, since their food laws forbid them to eat or handle pork. He was continuing down the wrong path. Then he came to his senses. He realized that even his father's servants lived better than this.

"I will set out and go back to my father and say to him: 'Father, I have sinned against heaven and against you. I am no longer worthy to be called your son; make me like one of your hired servants.' So he got up and went to his father. But while he was still a long way off, his father saw him and was filled with compassion for him; he ran to his son, threw his arms around him and kissed him." (Luke. 15:18-20)

65

On the road of life, sometimes we stray off the path God wants for us. When we stray, we are embarrassed to admit our mistakes. We may be ashamed of decisions we have made and the havoc they have caused. Then we come to our senses. We want to find our way back to the path God has chosen for us.

Here's the good news. Not only will God help you find your way home, but He will come looking for you. In another parable, Jesus told about the shepherd who left the ninety-nine sheep who were safe in the fold and went out looking for the one who was lost. If you are lost, just know that God is looking for you. He will show the way back, ready to forgive. Though we may have consequences to deal with, we will not have to face them alone. As the father of the prodigal son said to the brother, "We had to be merry and rejoice. This brother of yours was dead and has begun to live, and was lost and has been found."

CHAPTER 18

Stormy Weather

Driving can be challenging in the best of circumstances. On any average sunny day, you are likely to have your patience tried at some time. But throw inclement weather into the equation, and you have yourself real problems. You can quickly become afraid that you will lose control and harm yourself, your loved ones, and others on the road around you.

I remember vividly a terrible rainstorm I drove through with my son, Josh. He was going through a bone marrow transplant, and he and my husband, Chip, had to drive every day to the cancer center over an hour away on the crowded interstate. During those days, we had to watch him carefully for any signs of infection or fever since his immune system was wiped out from the strong chemotherapy he had received.

It had been raining all day, and the boys were tired from the long day of treatment and driving to and from the hospital in the storm. Around ten o'clock that night, Josh's temperature had risen to a dangerous level. We had been told to call the doctor at that point and hurry to the special bone marrow unit at the hospital. Chip was so tired from the long day in the driving rain, so I decided to take my turn. Josh and I made our way to the interstate with caution. The lights of the cars and trucks on the busy highway were distorted by the rain on the road and the windshield. I really couldn't remember driving in such heavy rain before. The wipers couldn't keep up with the sheer volume of water sloshing across the windshield. In fact, it got to the point that I couldn't make out the lane lines on the road. I was terrified, but didn't want Josh to know how scared I was. It was very quiet in the car. I had turned off the radio so that I could focus all of my attention on staying in the lane. I kept a constant prayer for our safety on my lips. "Please, God," I whispered. "Help me stay in my lane. Help me get to the hospital safely."

Every muscle in my body was taut as I gripped the steering wheel. I tried to feel the movements of the drivers around me, though I knew that wasn't really possible. The fear I felt made me concentrate on every little movement of the car. It was as if all of my senses were heightened including my awareness of God's presence and the precious life I was transporting. I knew that God was with me. Before long, I saw the exit to the hospital. As I left the highway, my speed slowed and so did my heartbeat. I couldn't stop thanking God for bringing us safely to our destination.

***

When storms come your way in life, you may have a feeling that hard times are coming. You may have been travelling down a bumpy road for a while. You may be tired from fighting to stay hopeful in a seemingly hopeless situation. Then, when you are in a weakened condition, you see the storm clouds brewing up ahead.

Matthew chapter 14 tells about a night when Jesus went up onto a mountain to pray. He sent his disciples ahead to cross the Sea of Galilee, telling them that he would join them later. During the trip, a storm began to brew on the lake, buffeting the boat. The disciples were afraid. But then they looked out and saw Jesus walking towards them on the surface of the lake.

"When the disciples saw him walking on the lake, they were terrified. 'It's a ghost,' they said and cried out in fear!' But Jesus immediately said to them: 'Take courage! It is I. Don't be afraid.' 'Lord, if it's you,' Peter replied, 'Tell me to come to you on the water.' 'Come,' he said.

Then Peter got down out of the boat, walked on the water and came toward Jesus. But when he saw the wind, he was afraid and, beginning to sink, cried out, 'Lord, save me!'

Immediately Jesus reached out his hand and caught him. 'You of little faith,' he said, 'why did you doubt?'" (Matthew. 14:26-31)

I'm not sure what Peter's motives were with this request. Did he really need Jesus to prove who He was?? Probably not. I think it was pretty obvious that it could be no one else. So what was he really asking? Jesus was showing His complete power over the forces of nature, proving once again that He was the Son of God. He could heal the sick, control the winds, turn the water into wine—things no one had ever seen before. But there was a different kind of miracle that Peter really had doubts about. Yes, he knew that Jesus was the master of all creation. But could he transform a simple man like himself? Could He reach inside Peter's life and change a rough, tough fisherman into a man after God's own heart?

I think that this is the question many of us have when it comes to God. It's not that we doubt His power. It's that we doubt ourselves. We doubt that God can re-create us and transform our flawed selves into a new creation. We see that, even though we try every day, we fall short. We can't resist temptation. We fail to love our neighbors and to live up to being what God wants us to be.

Jesus called Peter to come on out onto the water. At first he was doing it! He was walking on the water, too. But then he saw the storm raging around him. He remembered his weakness, and began to doubt. He took his eyes off the Savior and started to go down. He cried out for Jesus to save him. And Jesus said, "Why did you doubt?" He took Peter's hands and helped him back into the boat. The winds died away, and he was safe.

When we face the storms of life, we must remember that we won't make it on our own merit. It is the grace of God that gives us the power to walk above the storm, through the storm, and come out safely on the other side. Not by our might, but by His. We must have faith that God not only is the Master of the Sea, He can even calm the troubled waters in our souls by His power and His great love. We don't always have faith in ourselves, but God, our creator, knows that with His hand in our hand, we will make it through.

CHAPTER 19

Arriving Safely at Home

No matter how far you have travelled, it is always good to arrive at home. Whether you are getting home from a hard day's work or you have been on a week's vacation, seeing the familiar sight of home brings that journey to a close. It gives you the chance to reflect on the people you have encountered and the events that have transpired along the way.

As you approach home, your focus narrows from the open road to the details of your very own world. Your see your street, your yard, your house. You thread your way around other vehicles parked nearby. Neighbors might be walking their dogs or taking an afternoon run. Children might be playing in their yards or riding bikes in the street. If you live in an apartment, you may be pulling into a parking lot or parking deck where you slow to a creep, maneuvering around other vehicles and pylons.

Your attention narrows even further as you masterfully center your car between the lines of your parking space or slide into a garage filled with all sorts of equipment and other items stored there. You complete your shut-down checklist. You shift into park, turn off the radio and the headlights, and turn the key. You look for your phone, your purse and items you are taking with you into the house. What a joy! You are safely home!

What has happened to the stressed-out driver whose Christian charity flew out the window when faced with a myriad of challenges out on the road? Suddenly, you are yourself again—the loving, forgiving child of God that everyone knows and loves.

What was that mysterious force that came over you once you got behind the wheel? Why did the simple act of driving your car bring out the worst in you? Well, I have an idea what causes this phenomenon. To explain it, let's use...

The Flow Chart of Frustration vs Freedom

On the road you face   At home you find

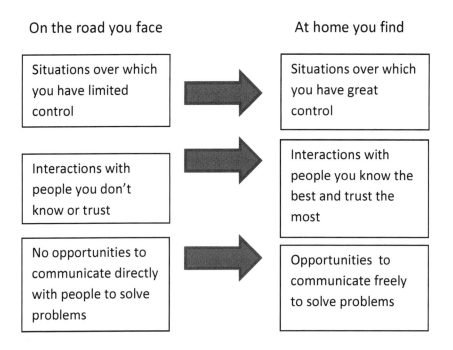

On the road you face	At home you find
Situations over which you have limited control	Situations over which you have great control
Interactions with people you don't know or trust	Interactions with people you know the best and trust the most
No opportunities to communicate directly with people to solve problems	Opportunities to communicate freely to solve problems

As soon as you get behind the wheel and shut the door, you venture out into the wide world of the unknown. As we have seen throughout this book, you will encounter the limitless situations that occur when thousands of people attempt to travel from one place to another. There is no reason or rhyme to the intertwining of their journeys. Most of the interactions are random, with only the intervention of a traffic light or road sign to interrupt the flow. Men have attempted to maintain some control to the chaos by enacting traffic laws and sending out patrol officers to monitor the mess. Though somewhat successful, they can only do so much.

As the Flowchart of Frustration versus Freedom shows, the "devil in the machine" is the lack of control. We all want to control our worlds. We want to know what is going to happen. When other people don't behave as we want them to, we want to explain to them the error of their ways. We know from experience that most other drivers cannot be trusted to use good sense and get out of our way. We want them to alter their inappropriate driving habits, and allow us to continue on our merry way without a hitch.

I once wished that I could let the other drivers I encountered know just what I thought about their crazy driving behavior. Perhaps by way of a bullhorn or of a scrolling electronic marquee stretched across my bumper. That would show them! But then again, maybe that would not be such a good idea. Better be glad that my thoughts are contained within the confines of my vehicle. Most of us have only gone so far as to lay on the horn or signal fellow travelers with a universal hand signal.

Once we approach home, the effects of the Flowchart begin to dwindle. We regain control of our world and return to the ones we love and trust. We are again in the presence of family and friends with whom we can communicate our questions and frustrations. The driving demons are dispelled.

***

In life, as on the road, we often are filled with fear and frustration when we encounter situations over which we have little control. Illness, addiction, loss of a loved one through divorce or death, a change in career or school, financial uncertainty and many other situations often cause us to lash out or "lose our religion." If we cannot talk about our problems with someone we trust, we feel alone and give in to despair.

That is why it is so important to always stay connected with the One who goes with us, no matter how far we roam. On the road or walking Through each day of life, if we speak with our Father each morning, breathe His name throughout the day, and thank Him for His constant presence when we lay our heads down at night, we will hear His voice reminding us of Jesus words:

"Be anxious for nothing, but in everything, by prayer and petition, with thanksgiving, present your request to God. And the peace of God, which surpasses all understanding, will guard your hearts and minds in Christ Jesus." (Philippians. 4:6)

The challenges of life are what make the world spin. Interacting with people and being God's light in each situation is what gives you your purpose. You are God's vehicle, speeding into the world each day, carrying His message of love. The next time you are behind the wheel, and that devil on your shoulder yaps in your ear, remember who you are and why you are there. Plug in to the source of your Life. Then you will know how to drive like a Christian.

SCRIPTURE REFERENCES

All Scriptures are from the New International Version unless otherwise indicated.

Chapter 1 Losing Your Religion

James. 3:8 But no human being can tame the tongue. It is a restless evil, full of deadly poison.

1 Corinthians. 10:13 No temptation has overtaken you except what is common to mankind. And God is faithful; he will not let you be tempted beyond what you can bear. But when you are tempted, he will also provide a way out so that you can endure it.

Chapter 2 Welcome to the Road

Deuteronomy. 4:29 But if from there you seek the Lord your God, you will find him if you seek him with all your heart and with all your soul.

Chapter 3 Distractions

Hebrews. 12:1-3 Therefore, since we are surrounded by such a great cloud of witnesses, let us throw off everything that hinders and the sin that so easily entangles. And let us run with perseverance the race marked out for us, fixing our eyes on Jesus, the pioneer and perfecter of faith. For the joy set before him he endured the cross, scorning its shame, and sat down at the right hand of the throne of God. Consider him who endured such opposition from sinners, so that you will not grow weary and lose heart.

Matthew. 22:37-39 Jesus replied: "Love the Lord your God with all your heart and with all your soul and with all your mind. This is the first and greatest commandment. And the second is like it: 'Love your neighbor as yourself.'"

Chapter 4 Pet Peeves

Ephesians. 4:1-2 …then, I urge you to live a life worthy of the calling you have received. Be completely humble and gentle; be patient, bearing with one another in love.

Matthew. 7:3-5 Why do you look at the speck of sawdust in your brother's eye and pay no attention to the plank in your own eye? How can you say to your brother, 'Let me take the speck out of your eye,' when all the time there is a plank in your own eye? You hypocrite, first take the plank out of your own eye, and then you will see clearly to remove the speck from your brother's eye.

Chapter 5 Fellow Travelers

John. 4:9-14 The Samaritan woman said to him, "You are a Jew and I am a Samaritan woman. How can you ask me for a drink?" (For Jews do not associate with Samaritans.) Jesus answered her, "If you knew the gift of God and who it is that asks you for a drink, you would have asked him and he would have given you living water." "Sir," the woman said, "you have nothing to draw with and the well is deep. Where can you get this living water? Are you greater than our father Jacob, who gave us the well and drank from it himself, as did also his sons and his livestock?" Jesus answered, "Everyone who drinks this water will be thirsty again, but whoever drinks the water I give them will never thirst. Indeed, the water I give them will become in them a spring of water welling up to eternal life."

Ephesians. 4:31-32 Get rid of all bitterness, rage and anger, brawling and slander, along with every form of malice. Be kind and compassionate to one another, forgiving each other, just as in Christ God forgave you.

Chapter 6 Bumper Stickers

Luke. 5:20-26 The Pharisees and the teachers of the law began thinking to themselves, "Who is this fellow who speaks blasphemy? Who can forgive sins but God alone?" Jesus knew what they were thinking and asked, "Why are you thinking these things in your hearts? Which is easier: to say, 'Your sins are forgiven,' or to say, 'Get up and walk'? 24 But I want you to know that the Son of Man has authority on earth to forgive sins." So he said to the paralyzed man, "I tell you, get up, take your mat and go home." Immediately he stood up in front of them, took what he had been lying on and went home praising God. Everyone was amazed and gave praise to God. They were filled with awe and said, "We have seen remarkable things today."

Chapter 7 Stuck in Traffic

Romans. 8:28 And we know that in all things God works for the good of those who love him, who have been called according to his purpose.
2 Timothy. 1:6 For this reason I remind you to fan into flame the gift of God, which is in you through the laying on of my hands.
Ephesians. 4:14-16 Then we will no longer be infants, tossed back and forth by the waves,and blown here and there by every wind of teaching and by the cunning and craftiness of people in their deceitful scheming. Instead, speaking the truth in love, we will grow to become in every respect the mature body of him who is the head, that is, Christ. From him the whole body, joined and held together by every supporting ligament, grows and builds itself up in love, as each part does its work.

Chapter 8 Curves Ahead

Luke. 10:36-37 Which of these three do you think was a neighbor to the man who fell into the hands of robbers? The expert in the law replied, "The one who had mercy on him." Jesus told him, "Go and do likewise."

Chapter 9 Intersections: Decisions, Decisions

1 Corinthians. 13:4-5 Love is patient, love is kind. It does not envy, it does not boast, it is not proud. It does not dishonor others, it is not self-seeking, it is not easily angered, it keeps no record of wrongs.
Matthew. 6:4 Then your Father, who sees what is done in secret, will reward you.

1 Peter. 2: 13-16 Submit yourselves for the Lord's sake to every human authority: whether to the emperor, as the supreme authority, or to governors, who are sent by him to punish those who do wrong and to commend those who do right. For it is God's will that by doing good you should silence the ignorant talk of foolish people. Live as free people, but do not use your freedom as a cover-up for evil; live as God's slaves.

1 John. 1:9 But if we confess our sins to him, he is faithful and just to forgive us our sins and to cleanse us from all wickedness.

Chapter 10 Stop and Go

1 Timothy. 6:17-19 Command those who are rich in this present world not to be arrogant nor to put their hope in wealth, which is so uncertain, but to put their hope in God, who richly provides us with everything for our enjoyment. Command them to do good, to be rich in good deeds, and to be generous and willing to share. In this way they will lay up treasure for themselves as a firm foundation for the coming age, so that they may take hold of the life that is truly life.

Ephesians 4:17-24 So I tell you this, and insist on it in the Lord, that you must no longer live as the Gentiles do, in the futility of their thinking. They are darkened in their understanding and separated from the life of God because of the ignorance that is in them due to the hardening of their hearts. Having lost all sensitivity, they have given themselves over to sensuality so as to indulge in every kind of impurity, and they are full of greed. That, however, is not the way of life you learned when you heard about Christ and were taught in him in accordance with the truth that is in Jesus. You were taught, with regard to your former way of life, to put off your old self, which is being corrupted by its deceitful desires; to be made new in the attitude of your minds; and to put on the new self, created to be like God in true righteousness and holiness.

Chapter 11 Sightseeing

Matthew. 25:34-36 Come, you who are blessed by my Father; take your inheritance, the kingdom prepared for you since the creation of the world. For I was hungry and you gave me something to eat, I was thirsty and you gave me something to drink, I was a stranger and you invited me in, I needed clothes and you clothed me, I was sick and you looked after me, I was in prison and you came to visit me.'

Ephesians. 4:11 So Christ himself gave the apostles, the prophets, the evangelists, the pastors and teachers.

Romans. 12:6-8 We have different gifts, according to the grace given to each of us. If your gift is prophesying, then prophesy in accordance with your faith; if it is serving, then serve; if it is teaching, then teach; if it is to encourage, then give encouragement; if it is giving, then give generously; if it is to lead, do it diligently; if it is to show mercy, do it cheerfully.

Chapter 12 Struggling Up the Hill

Matthew. 8:26 He replied, "You of little faith, why are you so afraid?" Then he got up and rebuked the winds and the waves, and it was completely calm.

Chapter 13 Maintenance

1 Corinthians. 12:12-20 Just as a body, though one, has many parts, but all its many parts form one body, so it is with Christ. For we were all baptized by one Spirit so as to form one body—whether Jews or Gentiles, slave or free—and we were all given the one Spirit to drink. Even so the body is not made up of one part but of many.

Now if the foot should say, "Because I am not a hand, I do not belong to the body," it would not for that reason stop being part of the body. And if the ear should say, "Because I am not an eye, I do not belong to the body," it would not for that reason stop being part of the body. If the whole body were an eye, where would the sense of hearing be? If the whole body were an ear, where would the sense of smell be? But in fact God has placed the parts in the body, every one of them, just as he wanted them to be. If they were all one part, where would the body be? As it is, there are many parts, but one body.

Chapter 14 Parking Lots

Luke. 4:43-48 She came up behind him and touched the edge of his cloak, and immediately her bleeding stopped. "Who touched me?" Jesus asked when they all denied it, Peter said, "Master, the people are crowding and pressing against you." But Jesus said, "Someone touched me; I know that power has gone out from me." Then the woman, seeing that she could not go unnoticed, came trembling and fell at his feet. In the presence of all the people, she told why she had touched him and how she had been instantly healed. Then he said to her, "Daughter, your faith has healed you. Go in peace."

Chapter 15 Fender Benders

John. 16:33 I have told you these things, so that in me you may have peace. In this world you will have trouble. But take heart! I have overcome the world."

Chapter 16 Speed Limits

Romans. 13:9 For the commandments, "You shall not commit adultery, You shall not murder, You shall not steal, You shall not covet," and any other commandment, are summed up in this word: "You shall love your neighbor as yourself."

Chapter 17 Directions

Luke. 15:18-20 I will set out and go back to my father and say to him: Father, I have sinned against heaven and against you. I am no longer worthy to be called your son; make me like one of your hired servants.' So he got up and went to his father.

But while he was still a long way off, his father saw him and was filled with compassion for him; he ran to his son, threw his arms around him and kissed him.

Chapter 18 Stormy Weather

Matthew. 14:27-31 But Jesus immediately said to them: "Take courage! It is I. Don't be afraid." "Lord, if it's you," Peter replied, "tell me to come to you on the water." "Come," he said.

Then Peter got down out of the boat, walked on the water and came toward Jesus. But when he saw the wind, he was afraid and, beginning to sink, cried out, "Lord, save me!" Immediately Jesus reached out his hand and caught him. "You of little faith," he said, "why did you doubt?"

Chapter 19 Arriving Safely at Home

Philippians. 4:6 Be anxious for nothing, but in everything, by prayer and petition, with thanksgiving, present your request to God. And the peace of God, which surpasses all understanding, will guard your hearts and your minds in Christ Jesus.

ABOUT THE AUTHOR

Terri Cox is a retired teacher and theatre director. She is the author of two books and numerous plays for children and adults. After a seeing the frustrations of friends, family and total strangers with their experiences behind the wheel, she applies her lifetime of Sunday School lessons to help you stay calm and keep driving.

Printed in Great Britain
by Amazon